The Coffee Book

The Coffee Book

Anatomy of an Industry
from Crop to the Last Drop

Revised and Updated

NINA LUTTINGER and GREGORY DICUM

THE NEW PRESS

NEW YORK
LONDON

Requests for permission to reproduce selections from this book should be mailed to: Permissions Department, The New Press, 38 Greene Street, New York, NY 10013

Published in the United States by The New Press, New York, 2006. Distributed by W. W. Norton & Company, Inc., New York.

Excerpt from *Brown Gold: The Amazing Story of Coffee* by Andrés Uribe reprinted by permission of Random House. © 1954 by Andrés Uribe.

Excerpt from *Stuff: The Secret Life of Everyday Things* by John C. Ryan and Alen Thein Durning reprinted by permission of Northwest Environmental Watch. © 1997 by Northwest Environmental Watch.

LIBRARY OF CONGRESS CATALOGING-IN-
PUBLICATION DATA

Luttinger, Nina.
    The coffee book: anatomy of an industry from crop
    to the last drop / Nina Luttinger and Gregory
    Dicum.—Rev. and updated.
        p. cm.
    Rev. ed. of: The coffee book / Gregory Dicum and
    Nina Luttinger. © 1999
    ISBN-13 978-1-59558-060-3 (pbk.)
    ISBN-10 1-59558-060-3 (pbk.)
    1. Coffee industry. 2. Coffee. I. Dicum, Gregory.
    II. Dicum, Gregory. Coffee Book. III. Title.

HD9199.A2D53 2006
338.1'7373—dc22
                                            2005058026

The New Press was established in 1990 as a not-for-profit alternative to the large, commercial publishing houses currently dominating the book publishing industry. The New Press operates in the public interest rather than for private gain, and is committed to publishing, in innovative ways, works of educational, cultural, and community value that are often deemed insufficiently profitable.

www.thenewpress.com

Book design and composition by Rob Carmichael, SEEN. This book was set in Adobe Caslon and Futura.

Printed in Canada

10 9 8 7 6 5 4 3 2 1

To our excellent families, and to David Kirkpatrick, father of this book

This coffee falls into your stomach, and straightaway there is a general commotion. Ideas begin to move like the battalions of the Grand Army on the battlefield, and the battle takes place. Things remembered arrive at full gallop, ensign to the wind. The light cavalry of comparisons deliver a magnificent deploying charge, the artillery of logic hurry up with their train and ammunition, the shafts of wit start up like sharpshooters. Similes arise, the paper is covered with ink; for the struggle commences and is concluded with torrents of black water, just as a battle with powder.

—Honoré de Balzac, *Treatise on Modern Stimulants* (1852)

Contents

Preface

COFFEE IS AN ANCIENT COMMODITY that weaves together a mosaic of histories dating back more than a millennium and stretching all the way around the world. Its story extends from the bustling cafés of sixteenth-century Cairo to the human misery of eighteenth-century Dutch colonial slavery, from the booming growth of Brazil in the nineteenth century to the modern-day coffeehouse imperialism of Starbucks. Much more than the mere chemicals that compose it, coffee is a bit of history itself.

And we consume it zealously. The world drinks about 1.5 billion cups per day—the United States alone drinks one-fifth of this. Coffee drinking is a cultural fixture that says as much about us as it does about the bean itself. A habit-forming stimulant, coffee is nonetheless associated with relaxation and sociability. In a society that combines buzzing overstimulation with soul-aching meaninglessness, coffee and its associated rituals are, for many of us, the lubricants that make it possible to go on.

Perhaps for this reason coffee occupies a distinctive niche in our cultural landscape. It is the major beverage besides alcohol to engender public houses devoted to its consumption (and both have done so since time immemorial). Uniquely, though, coffee is welcome in almost any situation, from the car to the boardroom, from the breakfast table to the public park, alone or in company of any kind. Since its adoption as a beverage, coffee has been offered as an antipode to alcohol—more so even than abstinence, perhaps in recognition of a human need for joyfully mood-altering substances and the convivial social interactions that go along with them.

Only a handful of consumer goods have fueled the passions of the public as much as coffee. The subject of ancient propaganda and the object of countless prohibitions and promotions over the centuries, coffee has inspired impassioned struggles on the battlefields of economics, human rights, politics, and religion. Coffee may be a drink for sharing, but as a commodity it invites protectionism, oppression, and destruction. Its steamy past implicates the otherwise noble bean in early colonialism, various revolutions, the emergence of the bourgeoisie, lopsided international development, technological hubris, crushing global debt, and more. These forces, in turn, have shaped the way coffee has been incorporated into our culture and economy. Colonialism, for example, served as the primary reason for and vehicle of coffee's spread throughout the globe; colonial powers dictated where coffee went and where it did not and established trading relationships that continue to this day.

The story of coffee also reveals how (and why) we interact with a plethora of other commodities, legal or not. Surprising similarities exist, for example, between coffee's early history and the current controversy over marijuana. Today's national debate over the merits of marijuana, although young by comparison, is the modern version of the strife surrounding coffee in other ages. The social acceptability of each has been affected by religious and political opinion, conflicting health claims, institutionalized cultural norms, and the moneyed interests of government and of private industry. The evolution of coffee's social acceptability highlights the delicate dance of interests and "truths" that governs the ways in which we structure our societies.

Coffee is consumed with great fervor in rich countries such as the United States yet is grown, with few exceptions, in the poorest parts of the globe. In fact, it was long one of the most valuable items of legal international trade, and it remains the United States' largest nonalcoholic beverage import by value. It is the principal source of foreign exchange for dozens of countries around the world. The coffee in your cup is an immediate, tangible connection with the rural poor in some of the most destitute parts of the planet. It is a physical link across space and cultures from one end of the human experience to the other.

The coffee-trading system that has evolved to bring all this about is an intricate knot of economics, politics, and sheer power—a bizarre arena trod by giants: by some of the world's largest transnational corporations, by enormous governments, and by vast trading cartels. The trip coffee takes from the crop to your cup turns out not to be so straightforward after all, but rather a turbulent and unpredictable ride through the waves and eddies of international commodity dynamics, where the product itself becomes secondary to the wash of money and power.

Even coffee drinks are not so straightforward anymore. While writing the first edition of this book we sucked down 83 double Americanos, 12 double espressos, 4 perfect ristrettos, 812 regular cups (from 241 French press-loads, plus 87 cups of drip coffee), 47 cups of Turkish coffee, a half-dozen regrettable cups of flavored coffee, 10 pounds of organic coffee, 7 pounds of Fair Trade coffee, a quarter-pound of chicory and a handful of hemp seeds as occasional adjuncts, 1 can of ground supermarket coffee (drunk mostly iced), 6 canned or bottled coffee drinks, 2 pints of coffee beer, a handful of mochas, 1 pint of coffee concentrate, a couple of cappuccinos, 1 espresso soda, and, just to see, a lone double tall low-fat soy orange decaf latte.

Since that edition of *The Coffee Book* came out in 1999, a lot has changed in the coffee industry. Vietnam rose from obscurity to become the world's second largest producer, contributing to a worldwide coffee glut that precipitated a crash in which wholesale coffee prices hit their lowest level in all of recorded history. The Coffee

Crisis wreaked havoc on millions of already impoverished farmers and forced the industry to reevaluate its role as a conduit between the richest on the planet and the poorest.

At the same time, the specialty sector—the gourmet coffee industry that began to flourish in North America in the 1990s—has become an even larger part of the overall coffee industry, with thousands of new players, each vying to distinguish itself in a crowded and competitive market. But even this sector's makeup is becoming more homogenized: half of all cafés in the United States are Starbucks outlets, up from just a fifth when *The Coffee Book* was first published.

For a century the industry lived and died by the benchmark New York "C"price, a composite that takes into account various commodity grades. But today, as traders and consumers increasingly consider origin and varietal, as well as the environmental and labor issues behind the coffee they purchase, the structure of the market is changing.

The growth of ethical consumerism has helped propel sustainable coffees—bird-friendly, organic, and Fair Trade coffees in particular—into the mainstream. Even large, mainstream coffee companies are dipping their toes into alternative approaches that help farmers and protect the environment, making some parts of the coffee trade at least bright spots in the otherwise dismal worldwide picture of heartless globalization.

Meanwhile, the rise of specialty teas and the emergence of energy drinks over the past few years has created new competition from non-coffee beverages.

And, since the first edition of this book, we've even managed to grow two magnificent, shiny coffee houseplants from Nicaraguan seeds. As we write this we're eagerly awaiting the ripening of our first crop of three fat cherries.

*   *   *

This coffee binge would not have been possible without the dedicated support of dozens of people, including Sarah Fan (second edition), Matt Weiland (first edition), and the rest of the crew at The New Press; TransFair USA; Mike Ferguson and Aaron Kiel at the Specialty Coffee Association of America; Joe DeRupo at the National Coffee Association; Robert Rice at the Smithsonian Migratory Bird Center; Ritual Coffee Roasters; Paul Katzeff at Thanksgiving Coffee; Rodney North at Equal Exchange; and the many coffee industry people who have been so helpful in providing us with information and opinions.

The Coffee Book

1

A Brief History of Coffee

The history of coffeehouses, ere the invention of clubs, was that of the manners, the morals, and the politics of a people.

—Isaac D'Israeli, *Curiosities of Literature* (1824)

The Social Drink

IN THE FAR REACHES OF ETHIOPIA'S FORESTED HIGHLANDS a knotted network of tree branches and tropical foliage creates a lush canopy over a forest floor brimming with life of all possible forms. Beneath the towering trees, smaller plants thrive in the dim sunshine peeping down from above. Where patches of this primordial landscape still remain, the scene has barely changed for millennia. But one member of this tropical ensemble has changed the scene everywhere else in the world. One dark, shiny-leafed plant, unremarkable among the wealth of understory greenery, has grown far beyond this ancestral habitat, sprouting up around the world, percolating through countless cultures and endless ages, and stimulating succeeding civilizations to thought and to action: coffee.

Used traditionally by nomadic mountain warriors of the Galla tribe in Ethiopia, where the plant is indigenous, coffee was first eaten as a food sometime between 575 and 850 C.E.—long before it was made into a hot beverage in 1000–1300 C.E. Originally, coffee beans were crushed into balls of animal fat and used for quick energy during long treks and warfare. The fat, combined with the high protein content of raw coffee (not present in the beverage), was an early type of "energy bar" (a recipe for *Bunna Qela*—dried coffee beans—found in modern Ethiopian cookbooks echoes this early coffee preparation: it recommends mixing fire-roasted beans with salt and butter spiced with onion, fenugreek, white cumin, sacred basil, cardamom, oregano, and turmeric). Concentrated nourishment coupled with caffeine had the added benefit of inducing heightened acts of savagery during warfare. Other tribes of Northeast Africa reputedly used the beans as a porridge or drank a wine fermented from its fruit. Its use seems to have been common and long-standing in its native range before outsiders began their torrid affair with the fragrant bean.

While the Galla and other groups who used coffee traditionally have their own stories of its origin, the Western myths of coffee's incorporation into our culture are variously divine or serendipitous and are closely associated with Islam. One well-known legend has it that coffee was discovered by a young Ethiopian goatherd named Kaldi (which means "hot" in ancient Arabic), who noticed his goats behaving frenetically after eating red berries from a nearby bush. Curious and hoping to energize himself, Kaldi tried some. To his delight, his tiredness quickly faded into a fresh burst of energy, and he began dancing about excitedly with his goats. The daily habit that Kaldi soon developed was noticed by a monk from a local monastery. The monk tried the fruits himself, and, noticing the effect, came upon the idea of boiling the berries to make a drink to help the monks stay awake during long religious services. News of the berry

Historic Timeline

1000	Physician and philosopher Avicenna of Bukhara is the first writer to describe the medicinal properties of coffee, which he calls *bunchum*
1470–99	Coffee use spreads to Mecca and Medina
1517	Sultan Selim I introduces coffee to Constantinople after conquering Egypt
1554	The first coffeehouses open in Constantinople
1570–80	Religious authorities in Constantinople order coffeehouses to close
1600	Coffee is brought into southern India by a Muslim pilgrim named Baba Budan
1616	Coffee is brought from Mocha to Holland
1645	The first coffeehouse opens in Venice
1650	The first coffeehouse opens in England, at Oxford
1658	The Dutch begin coffee cultivation in Ceylon
1668	Coffee is introduced to North America

drink spread rapidly throughout all the monasteries in the king-dom; the more zealous monks drank it to spend a longer time praying.

Another legend linked to Islam holds that the Angel Gabriel came to a sickly Mohammed in a dream, showing him the berry and telling the prophet of its potential to heal and to stimulate the prayers of his followers. In fact, Islam and the coffee bean seem to have spread through the Arabian peninsula during the same period, so it is perhaps not surprising that they are associated with each other. Subsequent antipathy toward coffee on the part of some Islamic authorities shows, however, that this identification was not absolute.

Kaldi dancing with his goats.

4

In what was to become a recurring pattern of introduction, early users valued coffee as a medicament more than as a beverage. Although some authorities date coffee's first cultivation back to 575 C.E. in Yemen, it was not until the tenth century that the bean was described in writing, first by the philosopher and astronomer Rhazes (850–922 C.E.), then by the philosopher and physician Avicenna of Bukhara (980–1037 C.E.). Referring to a drink called *bunchum*, which many believe to be coffee, Avicenna wrote, "It fortifies the members, it cleans the skin, and dries up the humidities that are under it, and gives an excellent smell to all the body."[1]

By the late sixteenth century, European travelers to the Middle East had described the drink in their travel journals, noting that it was commonly used as a remedy for a whole litany of maladies, particularly those relating to the stomach. During this time German physician and botanist Leonhard Rauwolf included in his travel journal from the Middle East one of the earliest European accounts of coffee and the already popular coffee habit he found there: "they have a very good drink they call *Chaube* [coffee] that is almost as black as ink and very good in illness, chiefly that of the stomach; Of this they drink in the morning early in open places before everybody, without any fear or regard, out of China cups, as hot as they can . . ."[2]

As Islamic law prohibits the use of alcohol, the soothing, cheering effect of coffee helped it to become an increasingly popular substitute in Islamic countries, particularly Turkey. During the sixteenth century most coffee beans were procured

1723	Gabriel Mathieu de Clieu brings a coffee seedling from France to Martinique
1727	Francisco de Mello Palheta brings seeds and plants from French Guiana to Brazil
1730	The English bring coffee cultivation to Jamaica
1732	Johann Sebastian Bach composes *The Coffee Cantata* in Leipzig, parodying the German paranoia over the growing popularity of the drink
1777	King Frederick the Great of Prussia issues a manifesto denouncing coffee in favor of the national drink, beer
1809	The first coffee imported from Brazil arrives in Salem, Massachusetts
1869	Coffee leaf rust is first noticed in Ceylon; within ten years the disease wipes out a majority of the coffee plantations in India, Ceylon, and other parts of Asia
1873	The first successful national brand of packaged roast ground coffee, Ariosa, is put on the U.S. market by John Arbuckle
1882	The New York Coffee Exchange commences business

1904	Fernando Illy invents the modern espresso machine
1906	Brazil attempts to increase world coffee prices by withholding some from the market through the "Valorization of Coffee"
1910	German decaffeinated coffee is introduced to the U.S. market by Merck and Co., under the name Dekafa
1911	U.S. coffee roasters organize into a national association, the precursor to the National Coffee Association
1928	The Colombian Coffee Federation is established
1930–44	Brazil destroys 78 million bags of coffee in an attempt to raise global prices
1938	Nestlé technicians in Brazil invent the first commercially successful instant coffee, Nescafé—still the world's leading brand
1939–45	U.S. troops bring instant coffee to a global audience
1959	Juan Valdez becomes the face of Colombian coffee
1962	Peak in U.S. per capita consumption: more than three cups per person per day

from southern Yemen, although a limited amount came from Ceylon, where the Arabs had apparently been cultivating it since about 1500. Mocha, on the Red Sea in Yemen, and Jidda, the port of Mecca, were the main ports for coffee export. Under the expansive Ottoman Empire of the Middle Ages, coffee, increasingly celebrated for more than its medical wonders, continued to grow in popularity and to reach a wider area. The drink came to be considered as important as bread and water and declared to be nutritive, refreshing weary Turkish soldiers and easing the labor pains of women, who were allowed to drink it. In fact, a Turkish law was eventually passed making it grounds for divorce if a husband refused his wife coffee. Eventually, the Turkish word *kaveh* gave rise to the English *coffee* as well as the French *café* and the Italian *caffè*.

By the mid-sixteenth century the drink had become so popular that drinkers in Constantinople, Cairo, and Mecca formed special areas in which to drink it: the world's first coffeehouses. Such establishments became centers for playing chess and other games, discussing the news of the day, singing, dancing, making music, and, of course, drinking coffee. Known as "schools of the cultured," these gathering places became popular with all classes and increased in number quickly.

The enthusiasm for coffee in this milieu would be startling even for the most committed modern coffee fiend. One of the earliest paeans to coffee was written in 1587 by Sheik Ansari Djezeri Hanball Abd-al-Kadir:

Oh Coffee, you dispel the worries of the Great, you point the way to those who have wandered from the path of knowledge. Coffee is the drink of the friends of God, and of His servants who seek wisdom.

　　. . . No one can understand the truth until he drinks of its frothy goodness. Those who condemn coffee as causing man harm are fools in the eyes of God.

Coffee is the common man's gold, and like gold it brings to every man the feeling of luxury and nobility. . . . Take time in your preparations of coffee and God will be with you and bless you and your table. Where coffee is served there is grace and splendor and friendship and happiness.

　　All cares vanish as the coffee cup is raised to the lips. Coffee flows through your body as freely as your life's blood, refreshing all that it touches: look you at the youth and vigor of those who drink it.

　　Whoever tastes coffee will forever forswear the liquor of the grape. Oh drink of God's glory, your purity brings to man only well-being and nobility.[3]

Despite its growing popularity, coffee remained a monopoly of the Arab world, and the secrets behind its cultivation were jealously guarded; foreigners were strictly forbidden from visiting coffee farms, and the beans could be exported only after boiling or heating to destroy their germinating potential. Nonetheless, increased travel by Europeans coupled with the steady expansion and integration of the Ottoman Empire slowly

1962	International Coffee Agreement establishes a worldwide cartel to control coffee supply
1971	The first Starbucks opens, in Seattle
1973	The first Fair Trade coffee is imported into Europe from Guatemala
1975	Brazil suffers a severe frost that sends coffee prices skyrocketing to historic highs
1989	International Coffee Agreement collapses; world prices plummet to historic lows
early 90s	Specialty coffee takes off in the United States
late 90s	Organic coffee becomes the fastest growing segment of the specialty coffee industry
1999	TransFair USA launches the first Fair Trade Certified coffee in the United States
2001–03	World coffee prices fall to their lowest real levels ever; millions of coffee farmers face a devastating crisis
2005	Specialty coffee represents half of the U.S. coffee market by value; Fair Trade Certified coffee is its fastest-growing segment

eroded the producers' capacity to maintain protective walls around this precious commodity; by the early seventeenth century monopolistic control inevitably began to crumble. A pilgrim from India named Baba Budan allegedly smuggled out the first germinable seeds from Mecca to Mysore around 1600. Not long after, in 1616, Dutch spies succeeded in smuggling out coffee plants that they eventually cultivated in their colonies in Java. Coffee was now in the hands of enough different interests to make its spread around the world inevitable.

Venetian traders, who had well-established commerce with the Levant, were the first to introduce coffee to Europe in the early seventeenth century. With coffee imported through the major ports of Venice and Marseilles, the first European coffee trade infrastructure took form. "Coffee is harvested in the neighborhood of Mecca," reported the *Paris Mercure Galant* in 1696. "Thence it is conveyed to the port of Jidda. Thence it is shipped to Suez, and transported by camels to Alexandria. There, in the Egyptian warehouses, French and Venetian merchants buy the stock of coffee beans they require for their respective homelands."[4]

In its early days in Italy, coffee was sold with other drinks by lemonade vendors and enjoyed by all classes. By the mid-seventeenth century at least some of the activity had moved into coffeehouses, described by the coffee historian William Ukers:

> The coffeehouse gradually became the common resort of all classes. In the morning came the merchants, lawyers, physicians, brokers, workers, and wandering vendors; in the afternoons, and until the late hours of the nights, the leisure classes, including the ladies. For the most part, the rooms of the first Italian caffès were low, simple, unadorned, without windows, and only poorly illuminated by tremulous and uncertain lights. Within them, however, joyous throngs passed to and fro, clad in varicolored garments, men and women chatting in groups here and there, and always above

the buzz there were to be heard such choice bits of scandal as made worthwhile a visit to the coffeehouse.[5]

Once coffee was in Europe, news of it spread, inspiring enterprising travelers and recent immigrants to import the bean. The first English coffeehouse opened in 1650, in the university town of Oxford, apparently by a Jewish man named Jacob. Increasingly popular among its natural constituency—students—coffeehouses (quickly growing in number) became regular meeting places for what were to become several of England's first social clubs.

Two years after the first coffeehouse opened in Oxford, an Armenian (or Greek, by some accounts) man from Smyrna named Pasqua Rosée opened the first London coffeehouse. Brought to London as a servant by a merchant named Daniel Edwards, Rosée served coffee each morning to Edwards's house guests, who grew in number over time, curious about the new

Frontispiece of King James I's *Two Broadsides Against Tobacco*, 1674. Early European coffee imagery highlighted the drink's exotic origins.

drink. The practice drew in so many visitors that Rosée, financed by Edwards, eventually opened a coffeehouse in St. Michael's Alley at Cornhill. The idea took off. In the years that followed, the explosive growth of coffeehouses served to firmly establish the beverage in England; by 1715 there were as many as 2,000 coffeehouses in London alone.

In England, doctors were some of the early staunch proponents of coffee, promoting the beverage for its supposed healing abilities. Some even considered it an effective remedy against the plague. In *The Virtue and Use of Coffee, with Regard to the Plague, and other Infectious Distempers* (1721) Richard Bradley wrote, "It is remark'd by several Learned Men abroad, that Coffee is of excellent Use in the time of Pestilence, and contributes greatly to prevent the Spreading of Infection. . . ."[6] Some went so far as to describe coffee as a medical panacea, as demonstrated in a 1657 advertisement printed in the old English newspaper *The Publick Adviser:*

> In Bartholomew Lane, on the backside of the old Exchange, the drink called Coffee, which is a very wholesom [*sic*] and Physical drink, having many excellent virtues, closes the orifice of the Stomach, fortifies the heat within, helpeth Digestion, quickeneth the Spirits, maketh the heart lightsome, is good against Eyesores, Coughs or Colds, Rhumes, Consumptions, Headache, Dropsie, Gout, Scurvy, King's Evil, and many others, is to be sold both in the morning, and at three of the clock in the afternoon.[7]

Public knowledge of coffee's pharmacological qualities greatly facilitated acceptance of the new drink and made the frequenting of coffeehouses seem almost virtuous in contrast to their alternative, taverns. To Puritans of the time, coffee was widely viewed as an answer to the rather widespread problem of public drunkenness, a natural result of the fact that beer was consumed with almost every meal. In 1660 James Howell wrote, "'Tis found already, that this coffee drink hath caused a greater sobriety among the Nations. Whereas formerly Apprentices and clerks with others used to take their morning's draught of Ale, Beer, or Wine, which by the dizziness they Cause in the Brain, made many unfit for business, they use now to play the Good-fellows in this wakeful and civil drink."[8]

The historian Michelet used stronger words to describe the transformation from alcohol abuse to coffee use:

> . . . For at length the tavern has been dethroned, the detestable tavern where, half a century ago, our young folks rioted among wine-tubs and harlots. Fewer drunken

songs o' night time, fewer nobles lying in the gutter. . . . Coffee the sobering beverage, a mighty nutriment of the brain, unlike spirituous liquors, increases purity and clarity; coffee, which clears the imagination of fogs and heavy vapours; which illumines the reality of things with the white light of truth; anti-erotic coffee, which at length substitutes stimulation of the mind for stimulation of the sexual faculties![9]

Coffee was also viewed by some as a healing solution to a more serious but still common addiction—opium. In 1785 Dr. Benjamin Moseley wrote, "Among the many valuable qualities of Coffee, that of its being an antidote to the abuse of Opium, must not be considered as the least; for as mankind is not content with the wonderful efficacy derived from the prudent use of Opium, the abuse of it is productive of many evils, that are only remediable by Coffee."[10]

But coffee's virtuous and healthful properties were only one reason coffee drinking became so popular; coffeehouses also offered a new form of entertainment that resonated with the Puritan ethic. A pamphlet published in 1675, *Coffeehouses Vindicated*, explained why many people began to prefer coffeehouses to taverns:

> First, in regard to easy expense . . . here, for a penny or two, you may spend two or three hours, have the shelter of a house, the warmth of a fire, the diversion of company. . . . Secondly, for sobriety. . . . Lastly for diversion . . . where can young gentlemen, or shopkeepers, more innocently and advantageously spend an hour or two in the evening than at a coffee-house? . . . it is the sanctuary of health, the nursery of temperance, the delight of frugality, and academy of civility, the free-school of ingenuity![11]

Typically situated on the second floor of a building, the first English coffeehouses had an atmosphere not so very different from those we frequent today. Early coffeehouses consisted of a single large room with several tables, allowing for the discussion of disparate subjects. Although coffeehouses developed reputations based upon their clientele (there were, for instance, distinctly business coffeehouses, complete with separate rooms for mercantile transactions), they were all open to members of every class—or every class that could pay for the privilege, at any rate.

This mixing of classes, so infrequent in other social venues of the time, was one of the characteristics that distinguished the coffeehouses as a means of entertainment: "The close intercourse between the habitués of the coffeehouse," wrote the historian Edward Robinson, "was to lead to something more than a mere jumbling or huddling together of opposites. The diverse elements gradually united in the bonds of common sympathy, or were forcibly combined by persecution from without, until there resulted a social, political and moral force of almost irresistible strength."[12]

Crowded with people from all walks of life discussing politics and cultural matters, coffeehouses became centers for urban social life—the drink itself fueling political discussion and, often, social upheaval. Accustomed to paying a penny to enter the coffeehouse and spend a good long while reading the papers and conversing with neighbors, the English nicknamed seventeenth-century coffeehouses "penny universities" for the inexpensive education they provided.

The arrival of coffeehouses at this moment in British (and more generally European) history provided a space within which the newly educated and active bourgeoisie could coalesce into a body of interests. In this way, the various scenes at coffeehouses embodied the zeitgeist of a place. "Coffeehouses provided [the middle classes] with a place for the interchange of ideas, and for the formation of public opinion," wrote the historian Harold Routh. "They were (although those who frequented them were not fully conscious of the fact) brotherhoods for the diffusion of a new humanism—and only at these foci could an author come into contact with the thought of his generation."[13]

Not surprisingly, then, coffeehouses evolved as early prototypes for the first social clubs and other social institutions created by the emerging Third Estate for their own organization and expression. The Royal Society, by way of example, is considered to have begun in 1655 as a regular gathering of students originally called the Oxford Coffee Club. The club met at Tillyard's, an early Oxford coffeehouse. One historical account describes the transformation from coffeehouse gathering to social club:

> The evolution of the modern club has been so simple that it can be traced with great ease. First the tavern or coffeehouse, where a certain number of people met on special evenings for purposes of social conversation, and incidentally consumed a good deal of liquid refreshment; then the beginnings of the club proper—some well-known house of refreshment being taken over from the proprietor by a limited number of clients for their own exclusive use, and the landlord retained as manager; and finally the palatial modern club, not necessarily sociable, but replete with every comfort, and owned by the members themselves . . .[14]

Lloyd's of London also evolved from a coffeehouse, one that primarily served seafarers and merchants. In his late-seventeenth-century coffeehouse, Edward Lloyd established a list detailing ships' cargo and their schedules. Underwriters came to his coffeehouse to sell shipping insurance and merchants came to keep track of the ships. From this tradition emerged Lloyd's of London, today one of the largest insurance firms in the world. Attendants at this institution are still called "waiters," as they were in the former coffeehouse three centuries ago.

If the English were swayed by the medical virtues of coffee and the sociability of their myriad coffeehouses, Parisians were finally won over for the sake of fashion. Already a favorite in Marseilles, the drink only became popular in Paris during the visit of a Turkish ambassador. Suleyman Aga spent 1669 at the court of Louis XIV

Lloyd's Coffeehouse in the seventeenth century. Patrons catch up
on the latest shipping news while others peddle insurance.

and was apparently single-handedly responsible for the French allowing coffee to take its place alongside wine as part of the daily liquid intake. When he arrived in Paris, he brought a sizable amount of coffee, and he introduced Turkish-style coffee to the numerous Parisians he entertained. During that year, the *haute société* of Paris fell under the spell of "Turkomania"—everything Turkish came into vogue. Of that period in Paris, Isaac D'Israeli wrote:

> A Turkish ambassador at Paris made the beverage highly fashionable. . . . The elegance of the equipage recommended it to the eye, and charmed the women: the brilliant porcelain cups, in which it was poured; the napkins fringed with gold, and the

Turkish slaves on their knees presenting it to the ladies, seated on cushions, turned the heads of the Parisian dames. This elegant introduction made the exotic beverage a subject of conversation.[15]

Writing *Le bourgeois gentilhomme* in 1670, Molière satirized the Parisian Turkomania as the extreme of absurdity and made fun of people trying to be Turkish simply by dressing like Turks and drinking Turkish-style coffee (which was, and remains, originally Arabic coffee). Little seems to have changed: modern Turkish coffee—ground to a powder with roast cardamom and thrice boiled in a long-handled *ibrik*—continues to have an exotic appeal to Western coffee drinkers, not to mention a powerful kick.

Although several small coffee establishments had opened in Paris earlier, Café de Procope was France's first enduring coffeehouse. Originally from Italy, Procopio Cultelli opened Café de Procope in 1689, directly opposite the recently established Comédie Française in Paris. The location proved successful; the café instantly became the meeting ground for actors, writers, dramatists, and musicians of the time.

Although in its heyday it had regularly hosted such famous patrons as Voltaire, Rousseau, Beaumarchais, and Diderot, the café lost much of its literary reputation after the French Revolution. Only in the last half of the nineteenth century, when bohemians such as Verlaine became regulars, did its hip reputation return, albeit temporarily. Today the café is a restaurant, but it retains the historic name.

Like the French, the Austrians also acquired the coffee habit from the Ottomans, but under very different circumstances. Although the Viennese had been introduced to the drink about two decades earlier, the city did not open its first coffeehouse until 1683, following the procurement of a rather unexpected coffee supply. In that year, when the Turks were defeated in battle outside of Vienna, they abandoned their supplies. These apparently included several thousand head of livestock and camels as well as several thousand sacks of exotic foods from the Middle East—several hundred of which turned out to contain coffee. While some speculated that the beans might be animal feed, a Pole named Kolshitsky was familiar with them from his travels to the Middle East and opened Vienna's first coffeehouse.

In fact, regardless of how coffee entered into use in a given country—as medicine, as vogue trend, as social happening, as stimulating drug, as temperance beverage, as exotic drink, as war booty—and regardless of the cultural norms and attitudes that it challenged, it always persisted and grew into a central part of day-to-day life. Once introduced, the popularity of coffeehouses and their proliferation served to institutionalize the coffee ritual and firmly establish its presence in European society.

Backlash to the Enfeebling Liquor

While coffeehouses served as the early social clubs of the time, the drink itself has seemingly galvanized drinkers to develop and act upon their own convictions. It was, for instance, from the Café Foy in 1789 that Camille Desmoulins led the mob that, two days later, brought down the Bastille. It was in a Boston coffeehouse in 1773 that American dissidents planned the Boston Tea Party. And it was in a New York coffeehouse at the dawn of the American Revolution that citizens convened a mass meeting in response to the battles at Lexington and Concord. "One of the most interesting facts in the history of the coffee drink," asserts the coffee partisan Ukers, "is that wherever it has been introduced it has spelled revolution. It has been the world's most radical drink in that its function has always been to make people think. And when the people began to think, they became dangerous to tyrants and to foes of liberty of thought and action."[16]

It isn't hard to see why any widely popular substance that made people clearly see their situation and the condition of their people was bound to become suspect to national and religious authorities and, by virtue of its enormous popularity, to be resisted by jealous business competitors. Coffee inevitably triggered a backlash. Even at the dawn of the first coffeehouses in sixteenth-century Islamic countries, pious Muslims began to protest because they felt the mosques were too empty and the coffeehouses too full. During this era distrust and uncertainty about the drink's effects, the freely spoken political and religious discussions, and the merry carryings-on at coffeehouses provoked the mufti in Constantinople to forbid drinking coffee by law.

Nevertheless, coffee drinking continued in secret, and coffeehouses were slowly reestablished. Coffee prohibitions were repeated several times in coffee's early Turkish history, and during one ban second-time offenders were allegedly sewn up in leather bags and thrown into the Bosporus. In sixteenth-century Mecca and Cairo, coffee faced similar prejudices and prohibitions, as religious intolerance and civil authorities occasionally intervened to suppress its popularity, though only temporarily.

Ironically, civil authorities often issued coffeehouse prohibitions claiming that they bred riotous mobs, when in fact the bans themselves created widespread public unrest. Strong public protests following any ban on coffee or coffeehouses always eventually won out; coffee was here to stay.

The early rise of coffee consumption in Europe in some ways resembled the tortuous path to acceptance that it had taken in the Middle East: religious fanaticism also briefly threatened coffee's future in Christendom and spawned its own semi-mythical appropriation of the bean. A legend holds that long before the first coffeehouse had opened in Italy in 1645 (and according to many accounts, several years before coffee had even been widely available in Italy) a group of priests in Rome appealed to Pope Clement VIII (1535–1605) to prohibit Christians from drinking coffee, calling it an invention of Satan. The priests claimed that coffee was given to Satan's followers, the Muslims, as a substitute for forbidden wine, and that Christians who drank it might lose their souls to Satan. Their plans were thwarted, however, by Pope Clement's discriminating palate. Tasting his first cup of coffee, Clement found the flavor quite agreeable and, reasoning that such an appealing elixir could not possibly be the work of Satan, opted instead to baptize it and make it a Christian drink.

The almost instant popularity of coffeehouses also naturally incited some antipathy from taverners, who saw a noticeable decline in their business. Not surprisingly, many of the early broadsides against coffee were written by them. One of the better known of these in England, *A Cup of Coffee: or, Coffee in its Colours*, was published in 1663, and begins:

> For men and Christians to turn Turks, and think
> T'excuse the Crime because 'tis in their drink,
> Is more than Magick . . .
> Pure English Apes! Ye may, for ought I know,
> Would it but mode, learn to eat Spiders too.[17]

But taverners were not the only jealous opponents of coffeehouses. In 1674 the popularity of coffeehouses incited women in England to protest with *The Women's Petition Against Coffee, representing to public consideration the grand inconveniences accruing to their sex from the excessive use of the drying and enfeebling Liquor.* Protesting their being left alone too much in the evenings (at the time in England, coffeehouses were not open to women), the women complained "that coffee makes a man as barren as the desert out of which this unlucky berry has been imported; that since its coming the offspring of our mighty forefathers are on the way to disappear as if they were monkeys and swine."[18] Later that year, the men answered with *The Men's Answer to the Women's Petition Against Coffee, vindicating . . . their liquor, from the undeserved aspersion lately cast upon them, in their scandalous pamphlet.* This hilarious piece of writing includes the following defense of coffee:

> Could it be Imagined, that ungrateful Women, after so much laborious Drudgery, both by Day and Night, and the best of our Blood and Spirits spent in your Service, you should thus publickly Complain? . . . But why must innocent Coffee be the object of your Spleen? That harmless and healing Liquor, which Indulgent Providence first sent amongst us, at a time when Brimmers of Rebellion, and Fanetick Zeal had intoxicated the Nation, and we wanted a Drink at once to make us Sober and Merry . . . for the truth is, it rather assists us for your Nocturnal Benevolencies, by drying up those Crude Flatulent Humours, which otherwise would make us only Flash in the Pan, without doing that Thundering Execution which your Expectations exact, we dare Appeal to Experience in the Café . . . the Physical qualities of this Liquor are almost Innumerable . . . Coffee Collects and settles the Spirits, makes the erection more Vigorous, the Ejaculation more full, adds a spiritualescency to the Sperme, and renders it more firm and suitable to the Gusto of the womb, and proportionate to the ardours and expectation too, of the female Paramour.[19]

In addition to competing business and gender interests, coffeehouses began to feel the heat from the king. Increasingly uncomfortable with the free and potentially seditious speech and association that characterized coffeehouses, King Charles II proclaimed their suppression at the end of 1675. Announcements were posted forbidding the operation of coffeehouses after January 10, claiming that, "in such houses . . .

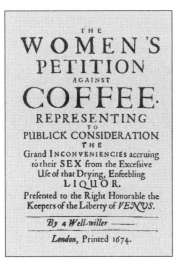

THE
WOMEN'S
PETITION
AGAINST
COFFEE.
REPRESENTING
TO
PUBLICK CONSIDERATION
THE
Grand INCONVENIENCIES accruing
to their SEX from the Excessive
Use of that Drying, Enfeebling
LIQUOR.
Presented to the Right Honorable the
Keepers of the Liberty of VENUS.

By a Well-willer

London, Printed 1674.

divers false, malicious, and scandalous reports are devised and spread abroad to the Defamation of his Majesty's Government, and to the Disturbance of the Peace and Quiet of the Realm; his Majesty hath thought fit and necessary, that the said Coffeehouses be (for the future) Put down, and suppressed . . ."[20]

Many protested against the decree, including the coffee dealers, who pointed out to the king that he himself earned good revenues from the trade. Within a few days the Crown gave up and reinstated coffeehouses, but with an additional tax and the condition that proprietors pledge not to sell pamphlets, books, or leaflets or allow speeches on their premises.

Whereas coffee's reputed healthful properties were widely known and facilitated England's ready adoption of the new drink, health was to play a slightly different role in France's early coffee history. Merchants who did business in the Levant had brought coffee to Marseilles in about 1660, but it was not until a few years later that a group of apothecaries and other merchants brought the first commercial shipment in from Egypt. By the 1670s coffeehouses had become quite common in the port city, and coffee drinking had risen dramatically. The physicians, who had earlier prescribed the drink as a medicament in keeping with contemporary medical opinion in Britain and Arabia, became increasingly anxious about growth in the coffee habit, since the now easily procured coffee might adversely affect their business. Breaking with their more sober colleagues abroad, the French doctors launched an attack against coffee reminiscent of the English taverners' smear campaign. In 1679 the physicians publicly denounced coffee, claiming it was poison and would disagree with inhabitants of the hot and dry climate of Marseilles. In a dispute held at the Marseilles town hall, the physician Colomb argued,

We note with horror that this beverage, thanks to the qualities that have been incautiously ascribed to it, has tended almost completely to disaccustom people from the enjoyment of wine— although any candid observer must admit that neither in respect of taste or smell, not yet of colour, nor yet of any of its essential characteristics, is it worthy to be named in the same breath with fermented liquor, with wine! . . . And why? Because the Arabs had described it as excellent. They had done so because it was one of their own national products, and also because its use had been disclosed to men by goats, by camels, or God knows what beasts! . . . the burned particles, which it contains in large quantities, have so violent an energy that, when they enter the blood, they attract the lymph and dry the kidneys. Furthermore, they are dangerous to the brain, for, after having dried up the cerebro-spinal fluid and the convolutions, they open the pores of the body, with the results

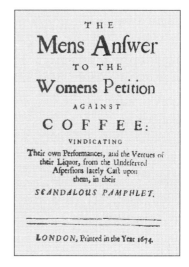

that the somniferous animal forces are overcome. In this way the ashes contained in coffee produce such obstinate wakefulness that the nervous juices are dried up; . . . the upshot being general exhaustion, paralysis, and impotence . . . For these reasons, we have to infer that the drinking and the use of coffee would be injurious to the inhabitants of Marseilles.[21]

But, in keeping with the general tendency of the public to ignore even the direst of medical warnings, especially when it comes to psychoactive drugs, people continued to drink coffee in coffeehouses and in the home.

In Germany, travelers such as Rauwolf had described coffee from journeys in the Middle East dating back to the late 1500s, but the first coffeehouse did not open until about a century later, around 1680, in Hamburg. Once introduced, coffeehouses spread quickly throughout Germanic lands. However, it took until about the latter half of the eighteenth century for coffee to enter German homes and gradually replace warm beer and flour soup at the breakfast table. The slow acceptance there was due in part to a general distrust of things considered "un-German," a long-standing national fondness for their locally produced beer, and ongoing prohibitions, taxes, and libel specifically directed against coffee.

These cultural currents are reflected in *The Coffee Cantata*, written by Johann Sebastian Bach in Leipzig in 1732, just as coffee was beginning to catch on for some and engender antipathy from others. One of Bach's secular cantatas, the piece is a sort of one-act operetta that lightheartedly parodies the increasing paranoia about coffee addiction—among other tactics, coffee opponents in Germany at that time urged that coffee should be forbidden to women on the grounds that it caused sterility. In the libretto (based on a poem by the writer Piccander) a father's obsessive concern about his daughter's coffee addiction has the daughter sing out defiantly, insisting, "If three times a day I don't drink my bowl of coffee, then in agony I'll wither like a dried-out chunk of roasted goat. . . . Ah! How sweet coffee tastes! Lovelier than a thousand kisses, sweeter far than muscatel wine! I must have my coffee, and if any one wishes to please me, let him present me with—coffee!"[22] Interestingly, Bach—apparently an avid coffee drinker—wrote the piece through his *collegium musicum*, an ensemble of musicians and professors who met regularly and held public performances every Friday evening at Zimmermann's, a famous Leipzig coffeehouse.

In Prussia and Hanover coffee eventually met with opposition for economic reasons. Noting the huge amounts of money flowing to foreign coffee merchants, Frederick the Great became increasingly critical of coffee, and in 1777 he issued a *Coffee and Beer Manifesto*, declaring:

It is disgusting to notice the increase in the quantity of coffee used by my subjects, and the amount of money that goes out of the country in consequence. Everybody is using coffee. If possible, this must be prevented. My people must drink beer. His Majesty was brought up on beer, and so were his ancestors, and his officers. Many battles have been fought and won by soldiers nourished on beer; and the King does not believe that coffee-drinking soldiers can be depended upon to endure hardship or to beat his enemies in case of the occurrence of another war.[23]

Frederick initially sought to ban coffee (in favor of chicory, a domestic substitute), but in 1781 the government realized how hard it was to enforce coffee prohibition. It was replaced by a royal monopoly on the drink, prohibiting roasting except in royal establishments. Private coffee roasting licenses were also made available to the nobility, clergy, and higher officials. Coffee supplies were purchased from the government, which served to increase Frederick's income substantially. Not surprisingly, such private licenses were not available to commoners, who could never afford them. The badge given for a coffee roasting license came to represent a sort of membership in the upper class, and commoners were forced to seek cheaper coffee substitutes such as barley, wheat, corn, chicory, and dried figs—or to procure it illegally. To help enforce the ban against roasting, disabled soldiers were often employed as "coffee sniffers" to sniff out those roasting without a license. Frederick had turned coffee into a drink of the nobility, a badge of privilege.

In 1784 another manifesto to ban coffee drinking among the lower classes was issued in Cologne, allowing it only for those who could afford to buy it in huge quantities—in effect making it available only to the wealthy:

To our great displeasure we have learned that in our Duchy of Westphalia the misuse of the coffee beverage has become so extended that to counteract the evil we command that . . . no one shall sell coffee roasted or not roasted under a fine of one hundred dollars, or two years in prison, for each offense.

Every coffee-roasting and coffee-serving place shall be closed and dealers and hotel-keepers are to get rid of their coffee supplies in four weeks. It is only permitted to obtain from the outside coffee for one's own consumption in lots of fifty pounds. House fathers and mothers shall not allow their work people, especially their washing and ironing women, to prepare coffee, or to allow it in any manner under a penalty of one hundred dollars. . . . To the one who reports such persons as act contrary to this decree shall be granted one-half of the said money fine with absolute silence as to his name.[24]

The anti-coffee police apparatus in the German states in this period closely parallels today's situation for illegal drugs. Any modern black marketeer would be familiar with the personal use provisions, drug sniffers, anonymous tip hotlines, and uneven, class-based nature of the German coffee laws of the late eighteenth century. The vehemence of the official reaction against coffee in these states as compared to other European countries stems in part from their lack of tropical colonies. The vested interests that arose in countries such as Great Britain, France, and the Netherlands over coffee production in their tropical colonies easily overpowered any objections to its consumption. Coffee, however, was already firmly entrenched in German habits, and it managed to survive the various taxations, prohibitions, and general suppression exercised against its use. Today, in fact, Germany is the world's third largest coffee consumer.

Colonialism and the Spread of the Bean

Beginning in the early 1700s, under the control of a handful of colonial powers, coffee cultivation increased dramatically throughout the tropics over the ensuing centuries. For most European colonial powers, coffee was a dream crop: a habit-forming, high-value tropical product that traveled well, with a ready market back home. Accompanying its expansion was a litany of cruelly inhumane and rapacious practices used for cultivating the bean, practices that indelibly scarred the landscapes and peoples unfortunate enough to be associated with the crop. Massive forest clearing and slavery were the seeming requisites behind growing coffee in virgin colonial lands, and the forces unleashed in this process have not yet played themselves out. Clearing forested land for coffee plantations continues today and slavery has, in many cases, been transformed into debt peonage.

Coffee production assumed a significant role in early colonialism as most of the major colonial powers became players: the Dutch cultivated coffee in Ceylon (now Sri Lanka), Java, Sumatra, Bali, Timor, and later, Celebes (Sulawesi) and Dutch Guiana (Suriname); the English grew coffee in the Caribbean and, later, in Ceylon and India; the French planted coffee in the Caribbean, South America, and later, in their colonies in Africa; the Portuguese produced coffee in Brazil, parts of Indonesia, and eventually in Africa as well.

The Dutch were the first to look toward colonial land with the intent of cultivating coffee. Although they had procured a coffee plant from Mocha as early as 1616, it wasn't until a few decades later, after they took control of Ceylon from the

Portuguese in the middle of the seventeenth century, that the Dutch began extensive cultivation in their Eastern colonies. Cultivation in Java began toward the end of that century, and by 1706 coffee beans had been brought to Amsterdam, along with a coffee plant for the Amsterdam Botanical Garden. Cultivation in the East Indies met with such success that for many years the Dutch East Indies controlled the price of coffee in the world market. Not surprisingly, the Dutch East Indies Company and local princes became fabulously wealthy as the growing world demand for coffee led them to put ever more land into production.

But success in the world coffee market was not without its price; for the sake of becoming a dominant coffee power, the Dutch brutally enslaved natives of their colonies. In 1676, Tavernier described the technique for capturing slaves:

> As soon as the inhabitants of these islands caught sight of the ships, as was their custom, men, women, and children ran to the shoreline . . . Each desirous of being the first to reach the ships. . . . Barely had they climbed aboard the ships [than] they were given such quantities of brandy to drink that they became intoxicated from the same: and the Dutch, having watched them getting into this state, immediately dispatched a large group of their people, armed with weapons onto the shore, and once they were on land . . . they bound and chained [them] and brought them onto the ships. . . . One can easily imagine the desperate cries which went up from these poor people as they were taken from their country in this fashion to Batavia [Java].[25]

Colonialism dictated where coffee was cultivated. A coffee plant from one of the royal French botanical gardens became the apparent matriarch of most of the coffee found in the West Indies and the Americas. Although accounts vary, this romantic, picturesque tale recurs in historical documents and has crystallized into the founding legend of coffee's New World provenance. In 1714 the Burgermeister of Amsterdam had given Louis XIV a present of a coffee shrub (actually a descendant of that first Dutch plant brought from Java to Amsterdam in 1706), which was planted in the *Jardin des Plantes* in Paris. Not long after, a French naval officer stationed in Martinique named Mathieu Gabriel de Clieu convinced the king's physician to secure him a cutting of the plant and permission to export it. Martinique, he was confident, would be a perfect place for France to cultivate coffee.

In 1723 de Clieu left Nantes to return to Martinique, transporting the coffee shoot in a glass chest so it could be brought up on deck each day and warmed by the sun. The journey proved treacherous: one of the men on board (allegedly with a Dutch accent) opened the frame and broke one of the shoots; the crew had to fend off pirates in a sea fight that lasted a whole day; a storm descended and shattered the chest; and the potable water supply on board ran so low that de Clieu was forced to share his own water rations with the plant. Nevertheless, the shoot survived to be planted in Martinique, and twenty months later de Clieu had his first harvest. Thereafter, coffee beans were distributed to doctors, intellectuals, and others of standing on the island. The islanders were quick to adopt coffee because, as luck would have it, the cocoa trees cultivated on many of these islands were doing poorly, due in part to a recent volcanic eruption and poor weather. Within three years, there were countless coffee shrubs on the island and the king had made de Clieu governor of the Antilles.

According to this account, coffee quickly spread to Guadeloupe and St. Domingue (Haiti) after de Clieu successfully cultivated it in Martinique. Nevertheless, some accounts maintain that coffee was already being cultivated in St. Domingue by about 1715, which would have meant that de Clieu could have saved himself the trouble of a trip to France and gotten his plants eight years earlier simply by taking a short trip there. Furthermore, the Dutch had already introduced the coffee plant to the Americas in about 1718, in Dutch Guiana. They had acquired this land in a trade with the British for their North American territories (including what later became Manhattan) in 1667, probably motivated by the coffee-growing potential in South America, and no doubt the lack of prospects in the frigid northern territory.

Regardless, the chain of consecutive thefts and deception continued, this time with the French as victims. A Brazilian lieutenant colonel, Francisco de Mello Palheta is said to have successfully brought seeds and plants from Cayenne, French Guiana, to the colony of Pará on the Amazon River in 1727. Acting as an intermediary in a boundary dispute between the French and Dutch in the Guianas, Palheta succeeded in smuggling out a coffee cutting disguised in a tremendous bouquet of flowers that had, ironically, been presented to him as a departure gift by the wife of the French governor (more romantic accounts hold that she actually hid it in the bouquet for him). Cultivation did not progress significantly until about thirty years later, however, by which time many kinds of coffee seeds and plants had been brought in from numerous regions. By 1800 Brazil was exporting its first coffee, an opportunistic response to a sudden change in the world supply and the first dramatic episode in the ongoing transformation of labor relations in the coffee industry: the Haitian Revolt.

French Haiti in the late eighteenth century had become the world's leading coffee exporter. Beginning in 1730, approximately 30,000 African slaves were imported each year to accommodate the needs of rapidly expanding coffee plantations. By 1791 Haiti was supplying half the world's coffee, cultivated with the labor of nearly half a million slaves. In 1793, two years after the suppression of the first uprising, the entire slave population revolted, destroying the island's plantations and estates and causing France to lose its position as a leading coffee producer.

While the Haitian revolt signaled Brazil's modest entry into the international market, it allowed Ceylon, under the British, to rise to global preeminence in coffee production. Beginning in the early nineteenth century, after the British took Ceylon from the Dutch, even more land was cleared for coffee—so much so, in fact, that in the 1860s Ceylon briefly became the world's largest coffee producer. Undertaking intense cultivation meant clearing tremendous tracts of rainforest. By 1869 approximately 176,000 acres of rainforest had been destroyed solely for the cultivation of coffee.

In that year, however, a lethal fungal disease named coffee rust quietly arrived on the island and within twenty years changed the balance of the world coffee supply. The disease spread insidiously: small, rust-colored patches on the underside of coffee leaves eventually became larger orange blotches. Over time the leaves would fall off, yield would decline, and eventually the plant would die. Since rust was not considered a serious problem at first, planters continued to clear land for coffee, bringing some 100,000 acres into cultivation in the following decade. Increased cultivation efforts had the unfortunate effect of masking the decline in crop yield caused by the coffee rust.

By the early 1890s the coffee rust had decimated virtually all of the coffee estates, an area of land estimated at over a quarter of a million acres. Coffee estates in India, Java, Sumatra, and Malaysia were also wiped out. But the switching of colonial commodities happened quickly; by the mid-1890s virtually all the coffee in Ceylon had been uprooted and the land replanted with tea.

The British East India Company had earlier and fortuitously laid the groundwork for this transition with its campaign for "the cup that cheers." Although coffee remained popular in England up through the latter half of the nineteenth century, the tea campaign, which began in about 1700, proved quite successful: between 1700 and 1757 average annual tea imports into England more than quadrupled to about four million pounds, and consumption continued to grow steadily. Thus, when the English replanted their devastated colonial coffee estates in Ceylon and India with tea in the late nineteenth century, the drink finally supplanted coffee as the beverage of choice among the British and became known as the national drink. A limited amount of colonial land continued to be cultivated for coffee, mostly in Jamaica, Uganda, and Kenya (the latter two in later years). Jamaica has cultivated coffee since about 1730, and since its early days, it has produced some of the highest-priced coffee on the market.

Just as Ceylon had been able to come to the fore in the coffee world following the internal collapse of the previous market leader (Haiti), Brazil emerged from the shadow of Ceylon's coffee-rust problem as the world's preeminent coffee power. Following independence from Portugal in 1822, the amount of land under cultivation in Brazil continued to swell, and production shifted to São Paulo, which turned out to be ideal coffee country. By the middle of the nineteenth century, Brazil was producing half of the world's 294,000-ton coffee supply. For the first time since the Dutch had wrested control of the trade from the Arabs, the leading producer was not a colony, although vestiges of the colonial relationship persist in the interactions between coffee producers and consumers even today.

By the dawn of the twentieth century, annual world production had reached one million tons, three quarters of which was supplied by Brazil. Brazil found itself in a position to replicate the policies of the original coffee exporters and began a series of initiatives to create a coffee cartel on a scale that dwarfed anything the Arabs were able to accomplish at the dawn of the original coffee era.

The Drink of the Modern Age

The ever-expanding supply of coffee and the vigor with which various producers pursued their interests did not occur in a vacuum, of course. Fueling this growth, and provoking deforestation, slavery, and profiteering, was the ever-increasing demand for coffee back in Europe and, later, North America.

Although Captain John Smith, founder of the Jamestown colony, was apparently familiar with coffee from his earlier travels in Turkey, no mention of coffee is found in records of his earliest North American colonial days. And, curiously, although the Dutch were already growing coffee by the time New Amsterdam (early New York) was settled in 1624, they did not appear to have brought any to the settlement. The year 1668 marks the earliest reference to coffee in North America, but by the end of the century coffeehouses had appeared in all the major cities.

The first license to sell coffee in the American colonies was issued in 1670 to one Dorothy Jones, in Boston. By the close of that century, the London coffeehouse and the Gutteridge coffeehouse were in business there as well. As in European cities, American coffeehouses quickly became centers for social, political, and business interaction. In contrast to their European prototypes, however, the American coffeehouses were from the start embraced by official organs. They occasionally hosted court trials in the long (or assembly) room, and often hosted general assembly and council meetings or special political events. In 1789, for example, the New York reception for newly elected president George Washington was hosted at Merchant's Coffeehouse by the governor and the mayor of New York.

New York's first coffeehouse, the King's Arms, opened in 1696 on Broadway near Trinity Church.

The first coffeehouse in New York—the King's Arms—was built and opened by John Hutchins in 1696, on a lot he bought on Broadway near the Trinity churchyard. The bottom floor of the coffeehouse was used for eating and coffee drinking, with booths separated by green curtains, while the second floor was used for meetings of merchants, colonial magistrates, and public or private business. This coffeehouse remained the only one in the city for many years.

Located in New York's growing financial district, Merchant's Coffeehouse opened in about 1737, on the northwest corner of the present Wall and Water streets (near the site of today's National Coffee Association headquarters). This coffeehouse became an important center for meetings and commerce; the Chamber of Commerce conducted sessions in the coffeehouse's long room, and, like Edward Lloyd, the proprietor eventually kept a marine list, announcing the names of vessels arriving and departing from the port. The proprietor also organized a register of citizens that may have been the first city directory.

Before it was destroyed in a fire in 1804, Merchant's Coffeehouse hosted a long list of momentous events, including the 1765 order to citizens to stop rioting over the newly imposed Stamp Act; the mass meetings after battles at Lexington and Concord; the birth, in 1784, of the first Bank of New York, the city's first financial institution; and, in 1790, the first public sale of stocks by sworn stockbrokers.

If coffee and tea were apparently both popular during the seventeenth century, how did coffee emerge as the hot drink of choice in the United States? The Boston Tea Party seems to have helped. When King George III issued the Stamp Act in 1765, angry colonists had protested "no taxation without representation" and both the Green Dragon, one of the most famous early Boston coffeehouses, and Merchant's Coffeehouse in New York became the scenes for planning boycotts of imported English goods. By 1770 increasing political tension about the issue caused the English to lift some of the duties that had been imposed—but the tax on tea remained. In 1773 citizens of Boston ("disguised" as natives) boarded English ships in the city harbor and threw the tea cargoes overboard, therein inspiring a lasting national affection for that other drink, coffee, which could be imported directly from French and Dutch colonies in the Caribbean. From that time, drinking coffee was viewed as a patriotic act, and drinking tea was seen as un-American. Curiously, then, whereas European colonialism seemed to dictate where coffee was cultivated and drunk, in the case of the United States, it was the end of colonialism, dramatically reflected in the Boston Tea Party, that marked coffee's rise to prominence.

The initiation of coffee as the American national drink in the late eighteenth century set the stage for a series of developments in the U.S. coffee trade that took place over the following two centuries—principally, the growth of a coffee trade infrastructure that served to smooth the flow of beans and bucks between producing and consuming nations. This infrastructure included the centralization of the coffee roasting industry, technological innovations facilitating higher yields, increasingly efficient transport mechanisms, and geopolitical developments favoring the growth of symbiotic relationships between the United States and key producing countries.

Later conglomeration of roasters into multinational corporations and the growth of Brazil and Colombia as the primary powers behind coffee production both echo some of the themes found in coffee's early European colonial history—namely, the ongoing struggle for monopolistic control and regulation of a sector capable of generating tremendous revenues and power. The attendant social and ecological costs of the commerce in coffee, however, were also globalized. Increasingly powerful, the roasting corporations eventually became nearly indistinguishable from government in matters of coffee as they worked closely together to ensure that trade agreements and policies aligned with their own agendas.

As the hegemonic power behind coffee consumption and its regulation in international trade, the U.S. government, too, has demonstrated its own particular flavor of imperialism. The United States has used its heft in global coffee consumption and the power of its big roasters to promote its own political agenda in coffee-producing countries. Geopolitical exigencies, such as the Cold War struggle against Communism in Latin America, have often been played out in the coffee arena.

Coffeehouses themselves have even assumed imperialist roles that harken back to early colonial history. When large retail coffeehouse chains such as Starbucks move into a neighborhood, they tend to take over the local coffeehouse scene—and, like a real colonial power, Starbucks' sphere of influence is spreading insidiously and growing richer all the time. Starbucks imperialism is already making inroads into Europe and Asia, spreading its own particular definition of good coffee, and homogenizing the once diverse coffeehouse experience.

Just as scientific innovation played a critical role in making the transition from energy bar to hot breakfast beverage many hundreds of years ago, research continues to play a vital role in changing consumption and production patterns. While scientific research has improved cultivation, processing, and transportation techniques and increased coffee varieties, flavors, and yields, research has also addressed the health impacts on consumers, pesticide impacts on growers, and the ecological impacts of cultivation. The results of such studies are instrumental in continually changing consumer preferences away from or toward specific kinds of coffees.

Coffee's more recent history also reflects developments in consumer tastes and consumer marketing more generally. Just as coffee's early adoption in Europe threatened taverns and may have reduced alcohol drinking, three centuries later the popularization of soft drinks and the appeal of its marketing image threatened coffee's appeal, particularly among young drinkers after the 1960s. In the 1990s the rise of specialty coffee has breathed new life into the drink. Today, the ongoing evolution of modern coffee consumption has become a blizzard of trade associations, branding and advertising, scientific research, marketplace choice, socially responsible coffees, and trendy coffeehouse chains. Quite an empire, built on a humble bush.

2

Coffee's Odyssey from Crop to Cup

The market price of a food product simply cannot provide the information needed to protect both the land and the people who farm it. It ignores vital information—the costs to land, soil, and human health—on which our ultimate survival depends.

—Frances Moore Lappé, *Food, Farming, and Democracy* (1990)

Bean Botanica

On the surface, it's pretty simple. Coffee is a plant. Its seeds are dried, roasted, ground, infused, and drunk. It's essentially the same as it's always been, at least since people started to drink it many centuries ago. But in the intervening millennium, and especially the past century, this simple process has become exponentially more complicated. Much of this has to do with technological innovation, but a good deal stems from a dramatic increase in the scale of human endeavor these days.

An estimated 20 million rural families depend on growing coffee throughout the world. Today, coffee is grown in nearly eighty tropical and subtropical countries and is one of the most valuable items of international trade.[1] In 2004 more than 25 million acres—an area about the size of Portugal—was used worldwide for coffee cultivation in order to satisfy the needs of hundreds of millions of coffee drinkers around the world. The United States has the highest coffee consumption of any nation on the planet, drinking roughly one-fifth of the 17 billion pounds of coffee grown worldwide in 2004. That amounts to approximately 270 million cups of coffee swilled each day in 2004, making coffee, with a retail value of $19.2 billion, the most valuable nonalcoholic beverage import to the United States. And all of this activity is the outcome of the thirst of millions of drinkers—every cup of coffee you drink is the product of two square feet of land under coffee cultivation—an area about six times the size of this book.

Transformation of the juicy cherries of a handsome tropical bush into one of the world's favorite beverages requires a series of steps that is as much about moving the beans from one place to another as it is about processing the ruby-like fruits. Coffee, grown in tropical regions of the world, must be carefully husbanded, then picked, removed from the cherries, dried, and bagged before it is even ready to leave the producing country. It is consolidated and shipped, and later it is roasted, blended, distributed, and eventually ground and brewed. A very sophisticated network that reaches to the farthest corners of the planet has grown up to supply this drug, and it all begins down on the farm, with the plant itself.

Coffee is a member of the genus *Coffea* in the family Rubiaceae. A woody shrub, coffee can reach thirty-two feet in height, depending on the species and growth conditions. In cultivation, however, it is usually pruned to about eight feet to facilitate efficient harvesting. The genus is found naturally in the tropical forests of Africa, where it is towered over by gigantic and dense canopies of magnificent trees. Not surprisingly, coffee cultivation takes place in parts of the world with geoclimatic features similar to those found in its native range: a lot of sunshine, moderate rainfall, altitudes

Botanical print of a coffee plant, showing flower, fruit, and bean.

between sea level and 6,000 feet, average temperatures between 60 and 70 degrees Fahrenheit, and freedom from frost.

The coffee plant is lush, with deep green, shiny leaves drooping like rows of flags along the sides of long, thin branches. In flowering season, fragrant clusters of small white flowers bloom out from the bases of these leaves. Following pollination, the flowers wither, and each is replaced by a fleshy fruit surrounding a hard seed, like a cherry (a drupe). Each "cherry" usually contains two seeds, or coffee "beans," although occasionally only one seed develops (called a "peaberry"). Once mature (some one to three years after planting), each tree produces approximately 2,000 coffee cherries per year, or about 4,000 coffee beans—the equivalent of one pound of roasted coffee. These green cherries take from seven to eleven months to ripen, depending on climate, species, and variety. When ripe, the cherries turn bright red and reach the size of small oblong grapes. Coffee bushes in full production sometimes bear flowers, green cherries, and ripe cherries all at once. Harvest seasons vary throughout the world, based on climate, elevation, and species.

Although there are more than twenty species within the genus *Coffea*, only two account for the vast bulk of the coffee drunk worldwide. *Coffea arabica* (known familiarly as arabica) is the original coffee—the bush revealed by the Angel Gabriel (or "discovered" by the goatherd Kaldi)—and is native to the highlands of Ethiopia. *Coffea canephora* var. robusta (known familiarly as robusta), is native to the hotter, wetter lowland forests of West Africa, and it entered the general commercial market only relatively recently, after World War II.

The 17 billion pounds of coffee grown worldwide in 2004 would form a pyramid with a base more than a thousand feet long on each side, and would tower to a height of more than 2,100 feet, distracting tourists from the decidedly lesser Eiffel tower (1,043 feet).

Top Coffee Producers

Source: FAO

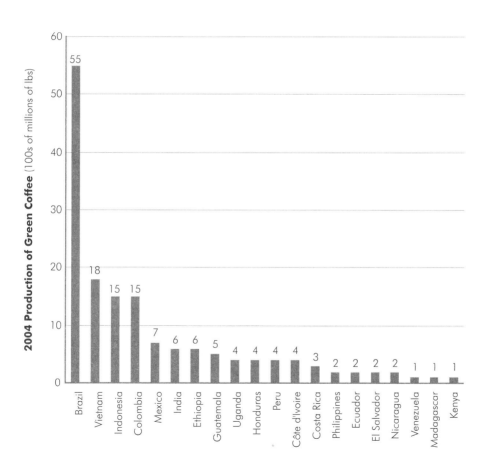

Area Harvested in 2004

Source: FAO

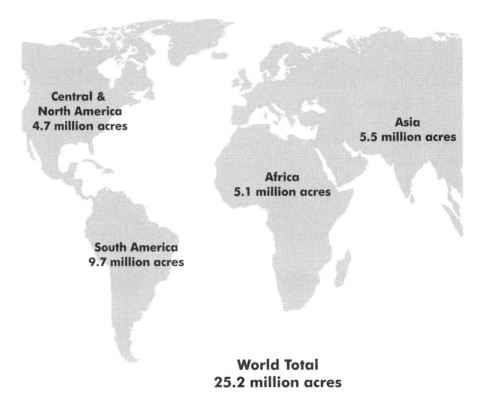

Central &
North America
4.7 million acres

Asia
5.5 million acres

Africa
5.1 million acres

South America
9.7 million acres

World Total
25.2 million acres

Arabica and robusta species differ in taste, caffeine content, disease resistance, and optimum cultivation conditions. Natural variations in soil, sun, moisture, slope, disease, and pest conditions dictate which coffee is most effectively cultivated in each region of the world. Generally speaking, East African, Central and South American countries grow arabica, and West African and Southeast Asian countries grow robusta, although these divisions are not absolute. The largest arabica producer, Brazil, is also the second-largest producer of robusta after Vietnam. Brazil grows just slightly more robusta than third-place Indonesia, which also produces significant amounts of highly regarded arabica.

C. arabica typically grows at altitudes between 1,500 and 6,000 feet, depending on location. Arabicas tend to be more susceptible than robustas to poor soils and diseases. Owing to this, and the fact that they are considered a tastier bean, arabicas command a higher price and are most often used in fine, specialty coffees and as a flavor component in robusta blends. Premium-quality, "washed" arabicas (which entail post-harvest processing in water) from northern Latin America trade at prices more than double those for lower-quality robustas or even "unwashed" arabicas. Today about 70 percent of our world coffee supply is arabica, Colombia and Brazil being the main producers.

In contrast to arabicas, robustas weren't cultivated until after 1850. Commercial production began on the West African coast between Gabon and Angola as European colonial powers (principally France and Portugal) sought to promote robusta cultivation and use in their home markets. This species grows from sea level up to 3,200 feet and tolerates warmer temperatures and higher humidity than arabica but is more sensitive to cold. Robustas tend to yield smaller beans than do arabicas, with an inferior flavor (but more caffeine) and a distinct bitterness. They are, however, easier to grow, as they demonstrate a wider tolerance to most diseases, soil conditions, and hotter climates. Following World War II, with attempts at national development through coffee cultivation in West Africa and Southeast Asia, robusta production grew and its consumption expanded (often without the knowledge of the consumer). With a harsher flavor and greater ease in cultivation, this variety commands a lower price in the market than arabica and is commonly used in both instant coffee and the mass-produced ground coffees seen in large grocery chains. Today most robusta is grown outside of Africa, where the only remaining top producer is Côte d'Ivoire.

Life on the Farm

Life on a coffee farm varies widely within and between countries. Coffee farms can range from small, traditional holdings with fewer than five acres to expansive, fully industrialized estates covering many thousands of acres. Coffee-farming families and migrant workers usually live on the coffee plantation itself, and the whole family is involved in maintaining, harvesting, and processing the crop. Although children in some coffee-producing areas can go to school (at least for several years), in the majority of regions most cannot because they are needed for help on the farm. Access to adequate health care is similarly missing for a majority of the world's coffee workers.

Although in some countries a few large concerns or landowners produce the bulk of a nation's coffee output, small-scale farmers collectively produce more than half of the global coffee supply. However, much of the processing, storage, and marketing infrastructure caters to the needs of the larger producers, and in many cases growing and processing facilities are owned by the same people. Small farmers and workers find themselves at the mercy of this system, particularly in those countries where coffee is the dominant crop. In such countries, rural people are left with few options, as the historian Tom Barry describes:

> So tenuous is the position of small coffee growers throughout Central America that they are more like contract employees than independent producers. While the large coffee growers can afford their own *beneficios* [mills], small farmers have no leverage in selling their harvest to the *beneficio* owners, since the coffee must be washed and dried prior to storage. These small growers are often forced to accept coffee prices that are 50 percent below the export value.
>
> It is common for the exporters to purchase an unharvested crop of coffee from a small grower at below market prices in exchange for an *anticipio* [cash advance] to allow the farmer to get through the year. "We are always losing right off the top," commented a small coffee farmer in Guatemala. "The rich growers finance themselves, and they can afford to buy Cherokee trucks and fly back and forth to Miami. But we [small coffee growers] can never get ahead."[2]

At the bottom of the pyramid of power in the coffee industry are the seasonal coffee workers. Crews of barefoot coffee pickers work from dawn to late afternoon filling basket after basket with red coffee cherries, which are then brought in bins to the *beneficio*. In El Salvador and Guatemala, entire families often labor in the coffee harvests. As one young Salvadoran mother named Julia explained to Barry, "You earn according to what you pick, so you have to bring a large family."[3]

Cultivation begins with carefully choosing beans from highly productive plants. The beans are planted and raised in nurseries for their first year, after which they are transplanted outdoors to the plantation. Whereas small, traditional farms will plant

A Latin American farmer examines his crop of fine arabica beans. Careful hand tending is crucial for the best results in the cup.

400 to 1,000 trees per acre (depending on location), large-scale modernized farms usually plant trees fairly densely—anywhere from 1,500 to 4,000 plants per acre.

Once planted, the coffee needs to be carefully maintained to protect against diseases and pests. In organic and most traditional cultivation systems, this means continuous weeding with a machete, applying mulch and compost around the plants, and introducing natural "beneficial insects" that eat pests. During the harvest season, handpicking begins early in the morning and lasts until evening. Pickers carry large sacks or baskets around their waists or throw the coffee cherries on tarps on the ground. As one visitor described coffee picking in Costa Rica:

We came to a place where there were workers harvesting the [coffee] cherries. There were many of them, whole families, ranging from toddlers still unsteady walking, to seniors old enough to be grandparents. . . . They used woven baskets a couple of feet deep and a couple of feet across. They tied these around their waists with rope. They had to crouch down, or get on their knees to pick the cherries. They used both hands. The wage was one dollar per full basket. The people work from five-thirty in the morning until six at night, seven days a week. . . . There are no facilities, no toilets or running water in the fields, and the people must bring food and drink and everything they need. As they fill the baskets, they empty them into large woven plastic sacks. When the sacks are full, they carry them on their shoulders to a place in the field where there is an overseer and a scale. The overseer weighs the cherries and pays the picker cash for them on the spot. Many of these people were Nicaraguans who had come, legally and illegally, to Costa

Rica for the coffee harvest. Others were Costa Ricans who worked part of the time harvesting bananas and part of the time harvesting coffee.[4]

The days are hot and long, the sacks of cherries are heavy, and the pay is usually astoundingly low—just a few dollars per full day in some countries, such as Guatemala. Wages for coffee workers vary widely, depending on the country, the scale of the farm, exchange rates, and the management structure. Even though slavery was abolished in most coffee-producing countries by the end of the nineteenth century, brutal forced labor and other exploitative systems have remained in some areas. Minimum-wage laws exist in some countries, but they are not always honored for impoverished, powerless coffee laborers. In wealthier countries, such as Costa Rica, wages may reach up to thirty dollars per day, but at the bottom of the scale, 96 percent of the workers in Madagascar do not receive cash wages at all but are paid in kind instead.

On large, modernized farms, common in Brazil, most picking is accomplished with the help of mechanical harvesters, monstrous machines that comb through the coffee plants, denuding them of all of their loose cherries but leaving the plants otherwise intact. Farmworkers on such farms must undertake regular applications of fertilizers, insecticides, fungicides, nematocides, and herbicides (sometimes containing known carcinogenic chemicals); perform standardized prunings; help work the machines; and conduct the post-harvest processing.

Because the need for labor on the coffee plantation is seasonal—peaking during the harvest—many regions have developed systems of migrant labor. Usually, these temporary laborers come from regions even worse off than the coffee-producing areas. Plantation labor in Guatemala, for example, is trucked to the coastal plantations from the impoverished highlands. Similarly, the Costa Rican harvest is undertaken largely by poor Nicaraguans and Panamanians. Sometimes the workers' homes are not so nearby: Hawai'ian coffee is often harvested by migrant laborers from Mexico.

Small-scale farmers with their own farms fall into a cycle of poverty, whereby their small production levels limit their access to credit, in turn hindering their potential for increased output. In the case of Mexico,

> Access to credit at market rates is not only difficult to obtain, but also very expensive. The possibility of getting it when you need it, rather than when the bank issues it, is remote. Due to financing difficulties at harvest time and a shortage of institutions that can attract local savings, producers have no cash flow throughout the balance of the farming cycle and are forced to use a line of farm credit for covering basic family expenses during the production phase, when it is available. And there is nothing more expensive than eating on credit with accruing interest. Besides, increased productivity on [five-acre] plots requires hiring additional labor for the coffee harvest. But, again, this cannot be accomplished without cash flow, namely, timely financing. And as if this were not enough, it is frequently the case that there are no roads . . . and increased production poses the challenge of transporting the product for rapid processing, but this cannot be done, of course, without the tools needed for the task. In a nutshell, they cannot produce more, because they cannot afford it, and they cannot afford it because they do not produce more.[5]

Lack of access to credit coupled with geographic isolation means farmers depend on middlemen to provide them with credit—at exorbitant interest rates—and to bring their product to market. Worse, land tenure systems in many tropical nations are stacked heavily against the rural poor. In those countries that endured colonialism, traditional indigenous land-tenure systems were supplanted by top-down structures that gave land rights to the government or to rich, often absentee—and often foreign—landlords. This state of affairs means that small farmers must pay for the use of their own land or be shut out from working their land entirely and serving instead as laborers for others.

Land reform has been a recurrent goal of development and workers' groups throughout the tropics, but the vested interests in these nations are unafraid to enforce their primacy by physically repressive means. Indeed, land inequity has been at the heart of many of the world's modern conflicts. In one of the most egregious of many such coffee-related conflicts, during the 1932 uprising in El Salvador—a time when 90 percent of the nation's economy rested on coffee—exploited laborers rose up against the coffee barons and their military henchmen, only to be brutally suppressed. In this *matanza*, some 25,000 peasants were slaughtered in a single week—a blood-bath that silenced opposition to the coffee regime there for the next fifty years.

Technifying Tradition

Coffee is traditionally grown in remarkably integrated agroforestry systems that incorporate many other useful plants. Holistic agricultural systems that structurally resemble coffee's natural forest habitat can provide small farmers with an array of additional crops and services. This kind of "agro-ecosystem" differs greatly from the endless rows of monoculture more familiar to most developed-world consumers. Vastly more diverse than fields of rippling wheat, traditional coffee farms resemble woodlots—but woodlots composed of carefully selected, useful trees, bushes, and herbs. Agroforestry systems have been developed over thousands of years to take advantage of the natural processes operating in a particular region. In many cases, traditional coffee farms have proven to be extremely productive and resilient, although not necessarily in the indicators measured by developed-world economists, who are most concerned with cash flow.

In traditional coffee farms, an overstory of valuable non-coffee trees shades the coffee bushes and provides a sort of insurance for small producers—a guard against risks such as frosts, violent storms, international market fluctuations, or social and institutional upheaval—all of which could adversely affect coffee earnings. The Smithsonian Migratory Bird Center describes these systems as resembling a forest,

> with coffee as the understory shrub, a mixed shade cover of fruit trees, banana plants, and towering hardwood species. . . . Such an agroforestry structure results in a fairly stable production system, providing protection from soil erosion, favorable local temperature and humidity regimes, constant replenishment of the soil organic matter via leaf litter production, and home to an array of beneficial insects that can act to control potential economic pests without the use of toxic chemicals. Traditional coffee, in fact, has been cited as [northern Latin America's] most environmentally benign and ecologically stable agroecosystem.[6]

The host of different non-coffee products grown alongside coffee provides the farming family with goods such as fruits, animal fodder, and firewood that they might otherwise have to purchase. At the same time, non-coffee products such as timber can provide farmers with alternative income. Some coffee farms have up to forty species of fruit and timber trees associated with them, including nitrogen-fixing trees that improve soil quality.

Owing to the drastic reduction in natural habitats around the world, agricultural land has become an important part of the natural ecosystems that surround and support human activities. In fact, the diversity of some wild animals in traditional coffee plantations reaches levels similar to those found in undisturbed tropical forest. In much of the world, natural areas are few and far between, and coffee agroforestry systems can maintain some of the habitat features required by native wildlife. In El Salvador, for example, traditional coffee plantations represent 60 percent of the country's remaining forested areas. In coffee-growing regions around the world, coffee "forests" cover a large proportion of the permanent cropland, providing critical woodland habitat where very few intact forest reserves exist.

Shade cultivation systems also have the advantage of demanding fewer chemical inputs than modernized, industrial-scale plantations, particularly because high crop biodiversity (many different species growing together) can enhance a crop's natural resistance to pests, and because the generational knowledge devoted to traditional coffee cultivation, passed down through succeeding farmer families, includes natural, nonchemical strategies for controlling such pests.

In contrast, larger coffee farms, such as the gigantic *fazendas* (estates) of Brazil, have always used little or no shade, and they produce the insipid bean that dominates the commodity market. Grown in rows that stretch to the horizon as a flat sea of luminous dark green, this sort of coffee is harvested mechanically, by machines that beat the cherries from the bush with long horizontal rods. By taking less care with each bean, such agro-industrial production yields an inferior product that sells for less but does so on a massive scale, which allows profit through volume. On the farms of the massive Brazilian coffee grower Ipanema Agroindústria, for example, 12.4 million coffee trees planted on 12,350 acres can produce up to 15 million pounds of green coffee annually in a good year, making this company the world's largest single coffee grower, with output nearly twice as great as Jamaica and Hawai'i combined.

While traditional smallholdings of less than 12.5 acres comprise more than half of the world's production, they are often marginalized within their nations' political and economic systems. In Mexico, 90 percent of the coffee is produced on such small-

Coffee Productivity

Source: FAO

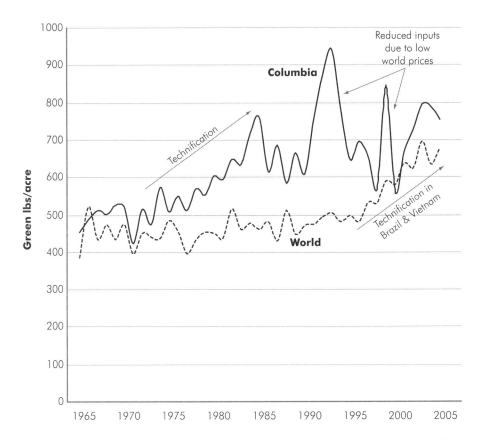

holdings, and 60 percent of the nation's growers are indigenous people who lack a political voice. Many of the indigenous people in the Chiapas uprising of the mid-1990s, for example, were traditional coffee producers. In many cases, ancient farming methods have been viewed as primitive and in need of modernization for the good of the farmers themselves, the sector, and the nation. Accordingly, when national governments turn their attention to coffee, they usually promote the more "scientific" or "technified" systems common on large plantations. For many governments, this approach has the added benefit of more tightly integrating indigenous or peasant farmers with the national economy by indebting them to banks and making them reliant on chemical companies, thereby restraining potentially dangerous community autonomy.

"Technified" coffee usually means the use of high-yielding varieties that grow best in partial or full sun. Conversion from traditional to "sun coffee" entails cutting down or thinning the valuable shade trees, destroying the added income and wildlife habitat benefits they provide. Technified coffee also demands more agrochemicals—pesticides, herbicides, fungicides, and fertilizers. The proliferation of technified coffee has led to a controversy over the benefits and harmful impacts of these new cultivation techniques. Complicating the issue somewhat is the fact that these two systems (technified versus traditional) do not represent absolutes—a gradient of cultivation techniques is used by farmers based on various economic and farm-specific factors, such as financial means, farm size, climate, location, coffee variety, and the local propensity for pest and disease problems.

The trend toward technification began in the 1950s. The agronomic Green Revolution swept aside thousands of years of traditional agricultural knowledge by promoting the development and cultivation of fast-growing, high-yielding varieties of grains (such as rice, wheat, and corn) that responded well to chemical inputs. Developing countries with cash-poor farmers eagerly switched to these new varieties (with the help of foreign development funds) and adopted new cultivation techniques that generally shifted away from traditional systems and included an increased dependency on agrochemicals.

While the Green Revolution focused primarily on grains, the craze for technological innovation in agriculture infected the world of coffee cultivation as well. Undertaken by the research institutions of coffee-producing countries, the development of technified strains was seen as a modernization that would help these nations achieve higher standards of living by increasing their coffee outputs (and hence their foreign exchange income).

Throughout the 1960s technification greatly expanded coffee production globally, as newcomers such as Indonesia, Angola, and Côte d'Ivoire got into the game and as the coffee output of small farmers worldwide increased—and production of locally consumed food, medicines, and materials decreased. By reducing the farmers' alternative income opportunities—traditionally associated with the fruitful shade trees—conversion to sun-coffee production also increases risk in the face of fluctuating coffee prices. If prices drop, these farmers have no backup income.

Adverse biological impacts become magnified as an increasing proportion of global coffee production is produced under technified systems. Sun or reduced-shade systems account for as much as 68 percent of Colombia's and 40 percent of Costa Rica's permanent cropland planted in coffee. About 40 percent of the land planted with coffee in Mexico, Colombia, Central America, and the Caribbean during the early 1990s has been converted to the technified system. This has caused significant tropical biodiversity loss, including the now-notorious decline of neotropical migratory songbirds such as Baltimore orioles, warblers, and vireos. These birds summer in the United States and migrate to different regions of Latin America during the winter, where they are heavily dependent on forested landscapes such as those provided by traditional coffee agroforestry systems. Indeed, studies have found up to 97 percent fewer bird species in sun-grown coffee as compared to shade-grown coffee.

Technified coffee not only reduces these shade tree habitats but also demands far more chemical input than does traditional coffee. Because they are produced industrially, these chemicals tie farmers to another risky global commodity: petroleum. Moreover, they introduce hazards that put workers and ecosystems at risk in new and dangerous ways. You can imagine the impact a coffee giant such as Colombia—with 68 percent of its coffee produced through technified cultivation—has on the environment and its coffee growers when, in a year marked by high international coffee prices, the country uses as much as 880 million pounds of chemical fertilizers. In 1994, that averaged more than a half pound of chemical fertilizers for every pound of green coffee produced in Colombia.

Many of the chemicals used in coffee cultivation, such as DDT, malathion, and benzene hexachloride, are banned in the United States for suspected carcinogenicity or persistence in the environment. Although tests conducted on green coffee beans by the United States Food and Drug Administration (FDA) in the 1970s and 1980s indicated the frequent presence of some of these pesticides, roasted beans remain generally clean. But while most of the chemicals don't find their way into our coffee cups—the beans are protected inside the sprayed cherries and at 500 degrees Fahrenheit the roasting process volatilizes any remaining chemicals on the outer bean coat—coffee workers and the ecosystem at large are routinely exposed to chemical

An Awful Lot of Coffee in Brazil (1930s–1940s)

The [Depression-era] planters sat upon their shaded patios and the *colonos* [tenant farmers] stood silent as the *ensaccadores* [baggers] prepared millions of bags of coffee for the journey to destruction. The crop was handled in the ordinary manner, for few planters could accept the fact that their coffee was worthless. It was picked, cleaned, dried, and transported as though destined to bring delight to the dinner tables of the world. But the sacks were hauled to designated locations for prompt destruction rather than to the port cities.

The burning centers were called *pilhas de incineração*. More than seventy-five of them worked steadily for over eight years. Huge, roofless sheds, they encompassed burning areas each nearly a half mile square. Thousands of tons of beans were mixed with heavy crude oil and set afire. They burned with a whining moan and exuded black and reddish flames. Over 2,000,000 bags were destroyed in 1931 and 9,000,000 in 1932. The crop in 1933 established an all-time record when almost 30,000,000 bags were harvested. Over 13,500,000 were burned. . . . The destruction of coffee continued in various ways until 1944. Coffee was burned, mixed with molasses unsuccessfully as cattle feed, combined with volatile petroleum and used for locomotive fuel, and thrown, by the tens of thousands of bags, into the sea. This last device was abandoned when the authorities discovered that the people were gathering and reselling the beans which washed up on the shore.

Chemists, scientists, and technicians were summoned and set to work to discover other uses for coffee. Briquettes of pressed coffee and fuel oil were developed for heating homes and industrial installations. The coffee bean was squashed, boiled, pressurized, steamed, strained and dried to a powder as science sought a use for the rejected crop. Vegetable oils, ammonia sulfate, caffeine and potassium sulfate were obtained from the beans, but none of the processes proved commercially feasible. A plastic made from coffee beans seemed at one time to promise a new

hazards. For instance, increased nitrogen fertilizer applications—a result of conversion to sun cultivation systems—have contaminated drinking water in many coffee-producing regions, and this sort of contamination has been implicated in certain cancers, birth defects, developmental problems, and other maladies.

The highly toxic insecticide endosulfan is commonly used in Colombia to combat the coffee borer pest known as *la broca*. The pesticide is banned in many regions of the world due to its acute toxicity and the frequency of worker poisonings. More than 200 human poisonings and four deaths were attributed to endosulfan use on coffee in 1993 and 1994—and these numbers are likely a gross underrepresentation, since such incidents frequently go unreported. Although Colombia has banned the pesticide and the nation's Coffee Federation supports its prohibition, the chemical is still used there.

Insufficient regulations concerning the type and amounts of chemical inputs, misunderstanding about proper application and safety procedures, lack of knowledge concerning environmental and groundwater contamination potential, and lack of enforcement authorities all contribute to serious health risks for coffee farmers. On the ground, the physical unsuitability of heavy equipment and gear for chemical applications—often designed in temperate climes—also interferes with proper worker safety.

Ironically, although technified farms outyield traditional shade farms (one study showed technified farms produced four times more coffee per acre than their traditional counterparts), the costs of the different production systems serve to shift the advantage in favor of the traditional farms. Comparisons of technified to organic coffee production have shown that the latter resulted in a significantly higher net revenue per acre, and the increased benefit is even greater when you incorporate the wide-ranging social and environmental costs of agrochemical-intensive production in the technified system.

These costs, which include the cleanup of polluted water supplies, the development of alternative sources of water, pesticide contamination, soil erosion, declines in local fish populations due to sedimentation and pollution, and the human costs to workers exposed to pesticides, are called "externalities" because they are not included in the production costs and hence are absent from the price. Rather, the burden of these costs is borne by others—local people, mostly. A systemic characteristic of the global economy, this problem was historically obscured by the existence of vast, thinly populated areas that could absorb our waste without overt ill effect. Now, with more than 6 billion people on the planet, there are few rugs left under which to sweep externalities. One of the long-term goals of many environmental economists is thus to internalize these costs by creating mechanisms whereby consumers pay to prevent these impacts from happening. The developing international system of carbon credit trading is one example of the fruits of this kind of thinking.

Regardless of its long-term ecological and social impacts,

industry to the planters. Named Caffelite, it was developed by crushing the beans to powder, adding various chemicals and then forcing the mixture under enormous pressure into a thin solid sheet.

An incalculable number of products could have been made with Caffelite, and funds were raised in São Paulo to build a pilot factory for its manufacture. However large-scale production proved impossible and the project was abandoned. . . . In fourteen years, more than 78,000,000 bags had been destroyed. But something more important than coffee had been ruined. The land had lost the faith of the farmers. The nightmare of the 1930s was unforgettable. Hungry, wretched and disillusioned, tens of thousands of small farmers and their families fled the farms to eke out a miserable life as wageworkers on the surviving *fazendas* [plantations] or in the coffee-poor cities.[7]

From *Brown Gold*, by Andrés Uribe, noted coffee scholar and U.S. representative of the Colombian Coffee Federation in the 1960s and despite mounting evidence against its economic advantage, the short-sighted trend toward technification continues. Aid organizations, including the United States Agency for International Development (USAID) and the International Monetary Fund (IMF), the original purveyors of the Green Revolution, have subsidized technification in Latin America with at least $80 million in "aid" since 1978. Only in 2001, in response to disastrously low coffee prices, did USAID shift its focus to quality improvements, sustainable production, income diversification, and improved access to credit for smallholder coffee producers.

Instead of providing poor farmers with a steady, higher income, crops such as technified coffee have encouraged unsustainable practices and have often dragged farmers into endless cycles of overproduction followed by precipitous price drops—all dictated by the whims of world coffee prices. Under these circumstances, their very lives are at the mercy of those with little regard for the small farmer—coffee-consuming nations, transnational corporations, and the governments of large producing nations—entities far removed from matters on the farm.

The International Travels of the Humble Coffee Bean

From the time they are planted, traditional coffee trees take from one to three years to bear fruit. During this period farmers must earn a livelihood growing other crops on available land, or, if cultivation techniques permit, generating income from products derived from shade trees. By the end of their life cycle of thirty to fifty years, coffee plants have exhausted their harvest potential and are uprooted, and the land is replanted with fresh plants. Yields peak at around fifteen to twenty years after planting and taper off toward the end of the life of a tree. Yields also alternate on a two-year cycle, with good (high volume) crops and then poor crops succeeding each other.

The unfortunate combination of growth lags, production cycles, and fluctuating international markets uniquely demonstrates the divergence between individual and group interests in the realm of coffee, and the consequences engender desperation for growers. When international coffee prices rise for one reason or another, farmers are encouraged to plant more coffee or to switch other crops to coffee. Because of the three-to-five-year lag time before production starts, prices have usually declined by the time these new plantings begin to produce. Worse, the new plantings stimulated by high prices everywhere else in the world are also coming on stream at the same time, and the glutted market results in stagnant or plummeting prices.

Because a coffee tree is a long-term investment, farmers are loath to uproot healthy trees, particularly young ones, so the situation remains one of grinding surplus and low prices until the next price shock. High prices usually last only one or two years, but low prices can persist for decades. This is the infamous coffee cycle, and everyone in the business is familiar with it. The industry has been struggling with the coffee cycle for more than a century, yet it continues because it is an inevitable result of the actions of millions of individual farmers responding to global coffee prices. Even the tightly controlled regime of international coffee agreements in the 1960s through the 1980s was unable to do more than dampen the cycle a little.

In turn, the cycle is driven by the finicky nature of coffee production—the alternating two-year cycle of good and poor crops combined with the vagaries of disease and weather. Good crop years produce huge surpluses, but poor ones can be devastating to a farmer—or a nation—while creating windfall profits for those lucky enough to be producing when a competitor suffers a frost, a drought, a heavy rainy season, or blight. In effect, any sort of major weather event in a major coffee-producing country causes a price spike, which stimulates increased production all over the world. A few years later, a period of low and stagnant prices invariably commences, as markets become glutted by overproduction.

Brazil, long the world's leading producer of coffee, has suffered from alternating periods of overproduction (relative to demand) and briefer, intense periods of reduced production due to frosts or droughts in coffee-producing regions. As a nation, Brazil has experienced the quintessence of the coffee cycle for well over a century, and its many efforts to smooth out the world market have met with mixed results, to say the least. For most of the past century, Brazil was more or less committed to regulating the flow of its coffee into the world market—even if it meant destroying huge amounts of it in an effort to keep prices stable. At various times during the last century (1906, the 1930s, and the early 1970s) the coffee giant had to destroy many millions of bags of green coffee, often by dumping it into the sea or burning it, to prevent a glut in the market. During the Depression and World War II, Brazil destroyed more than 10 billion pounds of coffee.

But times of surplus are only one side of the story. Brazilian arabica is grown in a part of the country that suffers rare but devastating-to-coffee frosts. Because a severe contraction of Brazilian supply amounts to a significant reduction in world supply, these frosts have profound effects on the world coffee market. Indeed, the coffee market is held hostage to a host of terrors, any one of which can drastically reduce world supply without warning. In 1975, for example, following a period of overproduction, the whole situation suddenly reversed after frost ruined much of the Brazilian crops, the Angolan revolution made deliveries impossible, and an earthquake in Guatemala, rains in Colombia, and disease in Nicaragua further hurt production.

Coffee prices worldwide skyrocketed, increasing fivefold between July 1975 and July 1977. In the United States, congressional hearings on coffee pricing were established, and there was a general suspicion of price-gouging among consumers. The prices reached in the mid-1970s remain the highest ever. Worldwide consumption patterns changed, and farmers—but especially traders—around the globe enjoyed windfall profits. Of course, the old predictable coffee cycle continued in its plodding pace, and, once Brazilian production recovered, prices fell again and entered another familiar stagnant period.

Even though this cycle is so predictable, consumers are always shocked when coffee prices rise but rarely notice when they fall. Each price spike is accompanied by worried newspaper reports and government inquiries in consuming countries—archetypal reports that read the same whether they come from 1907 or 1997. The rest of the time, coffee stays largely out of sight, with the miseries of the small farmers stuck in periods of low prices all but ignored by coffee drinkers who are able to enjoy savings of a few dimes on each pound of coffee. The coffee industry offers feast or famine, but, for the small producers, it is usually famine.

Cultivation is only the beginning of the long journey from crop to cup. After the cherries are picked, they must be processed, dried, bagged, and shipped, then roasted, ground, and finally brewed. For well-selected coffee, it typically takes about two or three months to go from coffee plant to roasting plant. At each step of the way, increased manual and mechanized labor, fuel, and chemical treatments serve to increase coffee's market value—unfortunately at the expense of increasing the negative social and environmental impacts associated with the bean.

The number of hands that coffee beans pass through on their way to your cup can vary considerably, depending on where the coffee was grown, how it was traded, and how it was subsequently processed. The wide variations in cultivation techniques make it impossible to generalize except at the coarsest level, although all beans go through the same basic processing steps: depulping, drying, sorting, grading, bagging, and roasting.

Beans are harvested through one of two methods. In strip harvesting, all the cherries—immature, overripe, dry, and ripe—are stripped off the tree by hand or machine. Strip harvesting works best in areas with only one harvest and relatively uniform ripening, so that the inclusion of quality-reducing unripe berries is minimized. The more common method, picking, consists of hand-selecting only ripe berries. This labor-intensive method is usually used in areas with steady rainfall, which leads to repeated flowering and fruiting throughout the year. Harvesting takes place in each field about once every month, and the greater care taken with each bean leads to better-tasting coffee.

Once the coffee cherries have been picked, they must undergo processing to remove the outer layers and expose the coffee beans inside. The slimy pulp of the fruit, a parchment skin, and the more delicate silver skin must all be removed. Depending on the availability of fresh water, two kinds of processing can be used: the "natural" or dry method and the "washed" or wet method. The processing method plays a large role in the final flavor and price of your coffee: the dry process tends to give coffee a full-bodied and mild aroma, and the wet process yields strongly aromatic coffee, with fine body and a lively acidity—properties that find it more prized in the market. Most arabica beans, especially the highest quality coffees, are wet processed.

This stage of processing can take place on the farm, if it is large enough to house the necessary facilities, or at mills central to a number of small farms. In some cases, processing facilities are privately owned, and coffee is bought from local farmers; elsewhere the facilities may be run by farmer-owned cooperatives or government agencies.

In the wet method, the cherry flesh is forcibly removed from the seeds by a mechanical pulping machine, usually within twenty-four hours after picking. Seeds are then dumped into huge fermentation tanks, wherein a twelve- to thirty-six-hour enzymatic bath loosens the slippery mucilage from the parchment on the seeds. Fermentation is an exacting science and is critical to developing the fruity acidity and aromatic flavors of the coffee; a single miscalculation can ruin a whole batch. Afterward, the loosened material can be washed easily from the seeds. The parchment layer remains attached as the beans (now called "parchment coffee") are left to dry for twelve to fifteen days in big, open sunny areas (called "patios" in English-speaking lands), where they are raked and turned over several times a day to ensure even drying.

In addition to the devastating impacts associated with deforestation to make room for coffee cultivation, post-harvest coffee processing—separation of the coffee beans from the cherry—results in dumping many billions of pounds of pulp into nearby rivers or into heaps in the open air, creating enormous fly-breeding piles of decaying, rotting fruit. In the rivers, bacterial decomposition of these tremendous loads of organic matter fouls the water and exhausts the aquatic ecosystems of oxygen, seriously impacting aquatic flora and fauna. Just in the 1993-94 Central American harvest season, for example, the production of 1.3 billion pounds of green coffee produced 6.8 billion pounds of pulp—about five times heavier than the coffee itself, and only a fraction of the many more billions of pounds of pulp dumped globally every year. Many organic and some traditional farms compost their pulp and use the finished product as a natural fertilizer for the crop, obviating the need for chemical fertilizers.

The dry method of processing is less expensive, less water-intensive, and less polluting, and is usually used for lower-quality beans. As its name implies, dry processing simply entails allowing the coffee cherries to dry in the sun for up to four weeks and then hulling the desiccated husks to reveal the beans. This method yields "natu-

Spreading Guatemalan coffee beans to dry in the sun after fermentation.

ral" coffees, characterized by a more heavy-bodied but more varied flavor than that produced by the wet process. Much of the Indonesian and Brazilian coffees and the traditional coffees of Africa and Arabia are processed this way.

Once dried, the beans are sorted and graded by size and density. These processes serve to unite similar beans (a hallmark of good coffee, and crucial to even roasting) and to remove unwanted material, such as defective beans, twigs, small stones, and leaves. According to many aficionados, the bigger the bean, the better the coffee—the largest being the prized Maragogype, or Elephant bean, a hybrid first identified in Brazil in 1870 but now more commonly grown in Central America. Grading differs from country to country; robustas are usually traded ungraded. Since beans of similar sizes can actually have different weights, the beans may be separated using a pneumatic process (depending on the scale of the operation) that uses an air jet to separate beans of different weights. A final hand-sorting process often takes place along a moving belt to prevent any stray "stinkers," "blacks," "sours," and "foxes" from contaminating the lot.

From the moment the arabica cherry is picked for wet processing, it takes up to fourteen days to become the green bean ready for commerce. The beans are then bagged in standard-sized 60 kg (132 lb) jute or sisal bags and stored in a storage depot at the port of the origin country. Then, in a process that has been likened to cask conditioning in beer and wine, the beans may be left for thirty to sixty days to acclimatize to their new (somewhat naked) condition and environment. Some beans wait in these warehouses for one or two years in an effort to regulate their flow into the market, although they tend to lose quality if stored too much longer. After this respite, the bags are shipped to destination countries.

Again, the exporting process can be undertaken in a number of different ways, depending upon the specific circumstances of the country of origin and the buyer. In some countries, coffee can be exported only by government coffee boards, while in others private exporters are the rule.

In 2004, total world production was just over 17 billion pounds of green coffee, and 70 percent of this was internationally traded. The 132-pound bags are shipped in containers holding about 250 standard bags each. More than a quarter of a

Decaffeinated Coffee

Decaffeination usually occurs at the roasting establishment in the consuming nation, prior to roasting, although in some instances the coffee may be sent to special decaffeination facilities in separate countries. Less than 15 percent of coffee consumed in the United States is decaf.

Decaffeination begins with the green bean. Early processes included steaming the beans to open them, soaking them in a solvent of noxious chemicals such as chloroform or benzene to destroy the caffeine, then steaming them again to eliminate traces of the solvent. Later, the coffee industry turned to methylene chloride. Although some of the big U.S. roasters have abandoned the chemical, the Food and Drug Administration allows its use in the United States as long as residues fall below certain limits. Nowadays, decaffeination can also be achieved using either a carbon dioxide process or a complex water process.

There have also been efforts to breed naturally uncaffeinated coffee, often using naturally occurring caffeine-free *Coffea* species, but flavor has been similarly absent. The modern hope is to create a bioengineered arabica that will have the full coffee flavor without any of the caffeine—in 1994 a California biotech firm patented such a creature, although by 2005 the researchers reported that they were "still working on it."

Instant Coffee

Of course, not all beans make it into your cup right after roasting. Some go through a much more sinister industrial process: dehydration. While preparations of pulverized coffee had existed since at least the eighteenth century and had been commercially available since their use as rations in the Civil War, modern soluble coffee was created in the 1930s by Nestlé technicians in Brazil. Their invention, Nescafé, was introduced to the market in 1938 and remains the world's leading instant coffee brand. Using a process of spray-drying adapted

million containers of coffee are shipped each year. The ocean trip from Central America to the United States can take as long as one month; trips from Asia or Africa can take twice that. Once in the destination country, coffee is subjected to an inspection by the consignee (buyer), to check that the quality and description of the shipment correspond to the exact order.

Cupping coffee, or professionally sampling the coffee to ensure quality, takes place at several points between the crop and the cup in both producing and consuming countries. Cupping is a revered art in the coffee industry. Seated at specially designed rotating tables, complete with spittoons and standard handleless porcelain cups, the cupper may sample scores of coffees each day. Small samples of freshly roasted, ground coffee are placed in the cups, then hot water is poured over the grounds, which float in a frothy slurry. Breaking this "crust" with a spoon, cuppers bring their noses to the coffee and inhale deeply, noting the subtle notes in the aroma. Next, they use a deep, round cupping spoon to loudly "slurp" a sample; loud slurping ensures that the cupper is creating a spray of coffee and air across the palate. Each sample is slurped twice in succession before the table is rotated and the next is tasted.

Coffee is warehoused in importing countries, usually in port cities. In the United States, coffee is stored chiefly in New York, Miami, Houston, and, until Hurricane Katrina destroyed much of that city's infrastructure in 2005, New Orleans. In 2005, just over 5 million bags of green coffee were warehoused in the United States at any one time. That's more than 650 million

Cupping coffee is taken very seriously, in spite of the chorus of loud slurps around the table. Here, Nicaraguan growers cup coffee with U.S. roasters to help improve quality.

pounds, or about 20 percent of the country's annual consumption. Though this coffee sits placidly in the bowels of vast warehouses, it can change ownership many times thanks to the constant churn of the coffee futures market.

Roasters usually maintain only a few days' supply at their plants, shipping coffee in from port warehouses or buying it from other importers as needed. As with virtually every other item of trade, the development of containerization since the 1970s has ended the picturesque days of long lines of stevedores loading coffee sacks on and off freighters. Now, some 80 percent of coffee is shipped in containers (although some purists gripe that the containers do not allow the beans to breathe in transit), and some, such as coffee shipped for Folgers, is transported without bags at all. Rather, it is blown into the container and sucked out again into silos once it reaches the roasting plant.

from their powdered milk facilities, Nestlé was able to create a product that became the emblem for the consumer-convenience movement that dominated industrial discourse in the era that followed.

While World War II saw a temporary slowdown in global coffee consumption, it also set off an instant coffee explosion. American soldiers were issued rations of Nescafé and (because wartime regulations had severely limited Nestlé's patent protection) Maxwell House instant coffee, thereby guaranteeing its success both in the United States and in liberated areas. Like the Ottoman armies that introduced coffee to Austria, the U.S. occupation forces around the world brought coffee to new markets, particularly Japan. Their other major contribution during the war was coining the term "cup of joe." The story goes that Admiral Josephus "Joe" Daniels banned the regular use of alcohol aboard ship, forcing the fleet to resort to coffee.

Following World War II, the popularity of instant coffee skyrocketed with the development of the freeze-drying process, which produces a cup superior to the older spray-drying method. The technique was further refined in the 1960s by extracting volatile oils from the roast coffee separately and adding them back to the vile powder following the removal of the water. Instant coffee was perceived as an exciting modern product, one that spared the consumer the bother of actually brewing a cup. That it also spared the consumer much of the flavor of coffee was beside the point—indeed, it was seen by the industry as the coffee of the future.

Though only 15 percent of coffee drunk in the United States is instant, it is popular in tea-drinking countries: 86 percent of coffee drunk in the UK is instant, and most of the growth on the coffee-drinking frontiers of China and Russia is in the form of instant coffee.

These technifications have greatly reduced costs and labor requirements and have contributed to a centralization of roasting capacity.

From the destination port, the coffee must be transported, via train or truck, to individual roasting houses. Since the beginning of the specialty coffee explosion, there has been a proliferation of boutique roasters, some roasting only a few hundred bags each year. In the United States, although an estimated 1,200 roasters were in operation in 2004, a small handful of large roasters account for the vast majority of coffee roasted. The large roasters are concentrated around the major coffee ports, and they often employ their own brokers to import green coffee directly from producers. In a further strategic risk-reducing move, the large roasters, like the producing countries, maintain large stockpiles of green beans. Small roasters, in contrast, buy green coffee from brokers who handle imports independently and who may or may not hold stockpiles. Thus smaller roasters, like smaller producers, are exposed to greater market risk, and they are more likely to suffer in times of market upheaval.

Roasting produces the primary flavor and aroma of your coffee. Green beans are usually roasted in capacious batch dryers, which spin and heat them evenly at temperatures reaching 550 degrees Fahrenheit. Heating the beans brings about several important chemical and physical changes: water boils off, starches convert to sugars, and sugars caramelize. When the beans get hot enough, they brighten, then turn yellow. Roughly halfway through the ten- to fifteen-minute roasting process, the beans turn tan and begin to "pop" much like popcorn, doubling in size. The heat is lowered. If the roaster desires a Cinnamon Roast, the process can end there. Otherwise, continued roasting will yield a City Roast, then a Full City Roast after nine to eleven minutes. Proteins slowly become denatured and turn into their constituents, peptides, which are exuded as oil onto the beans' surface as a Vienna Roast is reached. This coffee oil, or caffeol, gives coffee much of its characteristic flavor and aroma. If the beans are stored incorrectly after roasting, oxygen and light will cause the caffeol to become rancid over time.

About twelve to thirteen minutes into roasting, a second period of intense popping begins as the beans' cell walls begin to break down. At this stage the beans have become extremely dark and oily—an Italian Roast. The smoky flavor sets in, as bean sugars are now burning (carbonizing). At fourteen minutes, the second popping quiets, and the presence of blue smoke indicates the coffee has achieved a full-bodied, chocolatey French Roast. The dark, rich look of these beans can be deceiving: they are 20 percent carbon and no distinctive coffee varietal flavor remains, only the burnt flavor of the roasting process. Indeed, this roast earned its name because the French adopted long roasting times in an effort to burn away the unappealing bitterness of African robusta, a common import from their former colonies.

Throughout, a vigilant roaster carefully supervises the process by monitoring time, temperature, look, smell, and sound. From time to time, the roaster uses a "tryer" to pull out sample beans. At the end of the roast process, the beans have lost from 12 to 25 percent of their original green weight, depending on type of coffee and desired roast process.

Following roasting, a delicate process of blending may take place. Blending beans from different origins and roasts permits roasters to balance flavors and strengths, and, crucially for the large industrial roasters, allows the final product a consistent flavor even when bean supplies change because of changes in relative prices or availability. Mocha Java is a famous blend that has persisted through the centuries—since the days when Mocha and Java were the only coffee producers. The Arabian Mocha's mild acidity and fairly light body nicely balance the Java's heavy-bodied, deeper-toned flavors. For specialty roasters, blending is an art that helps create that perfect, distinctive cup; for industrial roasters, it is an art that helps minimize costs and spread risk in a volatile supply situation.

From this point, distribution depends upon the specific circumstances of the bean. Coffee at the large roasters is then ground and packaged, usually in vacuum-packed bricks or cans. For many specialty roasters, the goal is to roast their coffee in small enough batches so that it may be sold and drunk within a few days, thereby guaranteeing maximum freshness.

The progression from bean to cup can be so tortuous—and certainly covers so much physical distance—that its arrival in your mug seems almost miraculous. The high degree of organization required is a testament to the ability of the capitalist system to get things done—at least when there's the possibility of profit. Though choices in the marketplace are constantly changing to meet ever-evolving consumer tastes and preferences, for coffee, the basic steps from grower to consumer—cultivation, harvesting, processing, sorting, grading, bagging, shipping, cupping, and roasting—remain the same.

Modern technology, however, has refined most of the steps along the way, including the development of innovative cultivation techniques, decaffeinated and soluble (instant) coffees, processing machinery, shipping practices, and roasting procedures and equipment. While these changes have sometimes improved the flavor of our java, many of them have also served to increase the social and ecological impacts behind our daily dose. If there has been one consistent outcome of this system, however, it has been to make the international coffee-trading apparatus a very effective means for large corporations to make profits.

3

The Rise of the International Coffee Trade

Way down among Brazilians
Coffee beans grow by the billions
So they've got to find those extra cups to fill
They've got an awful lot of coffee in Brazil

—FRANK SINATRA, "The Coffee Song" (1946)

THE ECONOMICS OF THE INTERNATIONAL COFFEE TRADE involve astounding figures. Each year nearly 15 billion pounds of green coffee, or some 85 percent of the world's production, is traded between countries. In 2003, these traded beans were worth $5.5 billion—and that's just the core of the industry, the product itself. Tens of millions of people worldwide earn their living growing, processing, moving, or selling coffee, and hundreds of millions more enjoy coffee's energizing contribution to everyday existence.

A complicated network with a global reach has developed to move coffee from its tropical, developing-country homelands to consumers in wealthy temperate countries. As the global production of coffee is weather-dependent, much of the international trade mechanism serves to smooth out its "lumpy" supply, to reduce the risk to the industry of unpredictable changes, and to balance these changes against fluctuations in demand. Nonetheless, the underlying processes that govern this trade are little different from small-scale, coffee-cart economics—buyers and sellers at different levels of the coffee industry interact with one another for personal advantage, and all form part of a massive system that, miraculously, delivers this black elixir to your cup.

The story of coffee and the modern coffee system is a microcosm of the development of modern international trade. It is a tale of competing—and sometimes cooperating—interests engaged in a constant push-and-pull for power and its corollary, money. Brazil, Colombia, the United States, and the transnational food conglomerates are the principal actors who, through a century of the dance of commerce, set the stage for the coffee you drank this morning.

Brazil entered the twentieth century as a developing agricultural nation controlling at least three-quarters of the global production of coffee. Though it allowed the international market to set the price, this began to change even before the turn of the century as Brazilian coffee producers developed a political base.

In 1906 the producers achieved their goal: the manipulation of supply to increase coffee's market value—dubbed the "valorization of coffee." Brought about by a massive coordination of São Paulo coffee power and international financing that forced the hand of reluctant president Affonso Pena, valorization meant Brazil was no longer a passive participant in the global coffee trade.

Under this scheme, Brazilian coffee was released onto the international market through its Instituto Brasileño do Café (IBC), initially a growers' agency that was taken over by the government in 1926. The Instituto bought coffee from farmers, stored it in warehouses in Santos, New York, and Hamburg, and sold it on the world market. IBC intervention controlled the flow of Brazilian coffee, artificially reducing supply by stockpiling green coffee to sell during poor crop years. If this method was not sufficient to maintain good prices, the IBC destroyed coffee to further limit supply.

The program was quite successful for the Brazilian growers. Keeping 8 million bags of coffee off the market in 1906 led prices to their highest levels in over twenty years, and Brazilian foreign-exchange earnings increased substantially. For the first time, a mechanism for the regulation of coffee available to the international market was operating on the preponderance of the world's coffee supply. For the first time, one body was able to set the international price for coffee.

World Price for Green Coffee

Source: Ukers, ICO, FAO, NYBOT

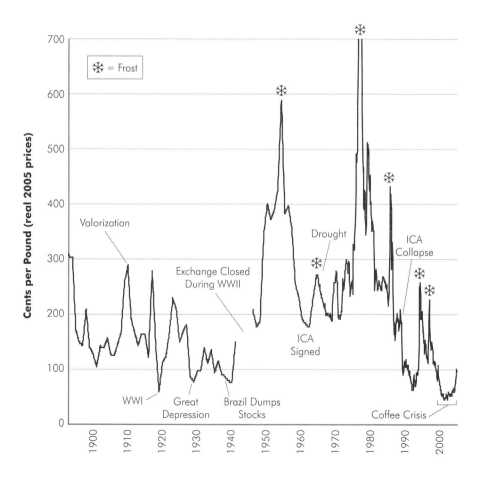

The repercussions for other producing nations were profound. In 1906, with the Brazilian valorization of coffee boosting world coffee prices, coffee fever struck Colombia. In a frenzy of settlement and development, reminiscent of a cross between the settling of the U.S. West in the 1860s and the boom of the Asian Tigers in the 1990s, Colombia underwent a period of unbridled growth and optimism (fueled, of course, by capital inflow, largely from the expanding coffee sector). Stimulated by the effect of the Brazilian valorization, thousands of peasants moved into undeveloped areas to start coffee farms. In the first thirty years of the twentieth century, Colombian coffee exports increased tenfold, and the power of the coffee sector became central to national politics.

In this climate, additional jumps in world coffee prices in the 1920s stimulated the creation of a new political force in Colombia: the Federación Nacional de Cafeteros (FNC). The FNC was organized as an industry lobby to represent the interests of the coffee producers, most of whom were smallholders. It enabled thousands of rural smallholders to participate in the political processes that controlled such critical features of their lives as infrastructure, tariffs, and interest rates.

The FNC very quickly became the antithesis of the Brazilian Instituto do Café. Where the Instituto sought to control world prices and protect an established sector by limiting supply, the FNC promoted unrestrained and aggressively expansionist trade in coffee. While the Instituto was inward-looking and more concerned with domestic control of supply to

The Colombian Coffee Federation (FNC)

Founded in 1928, the FNC quickly became a potent force in domestic Colombian politics. Its structure gives a unified political voice to an entire sector, and at times the FNC has operated as though it were an independent coffee government—establishing export, marketing, and structural policies that, while beneficial for its coffee grower members, were at odds with the goals of the rest of the nation. Throughout its history the FNC has been engaged in power struggles with Colombia's governments and political parties, at times influencing the direction of the nation's political history.

The FNC has been a powerful voice for coffee growers and has supplied its members with agricultural extension services as well as more basic infrastructure—roads, schools, and hospitals—from its early days.

Abroad, its efforts culminated in the creation of Colombian coffee as an origin in the marketplace. While advertising for Colombian coffee began in 1930, it was not until 1959 that Juan Valdez—the worldwide face of coffee—was created. The FNC has been able to create consumer demand for its coffee even though it does not market it directly. This shrewd meta-branding ensures that its real customers—the giant coffee roasters—cannot use cheaper substitutes if they hope to maintain the FNC logo.

This campaign has been wildly successful—Juan Valdez ranks with the Marlboro Man in consumer awareness, and has been through two incarnations (from 1969 to 2001 Juan was played by Colombian actor Carlos Sanchez, who actually owns a weekend coffee farm. Patterned on the rustic Colombian smallholder, Juan Valdez and his mule are the popular image of coffee cultivation in consuming countries, although lately his significance has become more iconic, as he has taken up surfing, hang gliding, snowboarding, and figure skating—pastimes not ordinarily practiced by coffee cultivators and their beasts of burden. Although for many years the FNC devoted millions of dollars to advertising in consuming countries, since

established markets, the FNC was resolutely cosmopolitan and sought to stimulate demand—particularly demand for Colombian coffee. In 1930 it began a campaign to brand its coffee, the forerunner of the Juan Valdez ads. The FNC contracted advertising agencies throughout Europe to promote Colombian coffee with the slogan "Buy Colombian when buying coffee." The idea of "Colombian coffee" very quickly became associated with high-quality coffee throughout the industrialized world.

At the same time, the FNC developed a network of operatives to monitor the world in which Colombian coffee hoped to compete. This network included researchers placed in New York and London to monitor and analyze the international trade and marketing of coffee, as well as spies to keep an eye on its competition (particularly in Brazil, where the Colombian consul was an FNC agent).

Domestically, the FNC promoted and eventually funded the development of an efficient coffee industry. Indeed, it eventually assumed the functions of government in the coffee sector, providing agronomic extension, financing, and directing regional development. Internationally, it was on a collision course with the Instituto do Café and the government of Brazil.

To this point, Colombian coffee producers had been "free riders" on Brazil. They had enjoyed the benefits of the Brazilian policies of coffee price support without investing in these supports in any way. They suffered no production limitations while the Brazilians withheld coffee from the market. As Colombian production continued to grow, this became more than just annoying to the Brazilians; they had to withhold more and more coffee in order to maintain prices—to "defend" coffee—only to see their work partially undone by unconstrained Colombian exports.

In Brazil the political power of the coffee growers was sufficient to continue the program of buying surplus coffee rather than let it rot on the trees in the terrible market of the Depression. This amounted to a massive subsidy to the growers; because production so greatly exceeded foreseeable demand, the Instituto had to destroy the surplus. Such an expensive proposition put Brazil in the position of supporting the global price of coffee single-handedly, by destroying one-third of its harvested coffee crop between 1931 and 1939—nearly 80 million bags, equivalent to almost three years' global consumption during that decade.

Beginning in 1931, Brazil sought to bring Colombia into its system of price supports by proposing agreements that would enable the countries to coordinate the sale of their exports. These overtures initially met with categorical refusal from the FNC, but, by 1936, after a vicious power struggle within Colombia, the two nations agreed to work in concert to maintain a constant price spread between their principal coffees. Almost immediately, some of the worst fears of the FNC were realized.

The FNC, under its obligations to Brazil, began to buy Colombian coffee to support its price. The international price of coffee rose, causing competitors in Central America, Africa, and

the Coffee Crisis its budget has been greatly reduced.

Since 2003, the organization has focused on the launch of a Juan Valdez café chain, which now has several locations in Colombia, New York, and Seattle, with plans for Boston and beyond.

Asia to increase their shipments, which obliged the FNC to buy still more of its own coffee. Speculators jumped right in, canceling orders from Colombia and even going so far as to sell coffee to the FNC, hoping to be able to buy it back later, once the FNC was forced to drop its supports and renege on the agreement. The FNC at this point must have developed a new sympathy for what it had been doing to the Brazilians.

The entire accord collapsed in June 1937, at a meeting in Havana. During the confusion, the FNC regained much of its independence from the Colombian government and resumed its policy of market competition, which exacerbated the crisis by provoking a trade war with Brazil.

Brazil reacted by dumping its massive coffee stocks into the global market, an action that severely punished all coffee producers by collapsing world prices. Things might have started all over again from this point, had there not been a second, untimely contraction of demand: the outbreak of World War II.

A New World Order

Jolted by the price war with Brazil and threatened by the loss of European markets, which had consumed nearly 40 percent of Latin American coffee exports before the war, the FNC quickly returned to the table. This time the goal was a binding trilateral agreement with Brazil and the United States that divided the latter's market between Brazil and Colombia.

The Inter-American Coffee Agreement (IACA) that resulted from this process in 1940 lasted through the war and was the operating structure for the international coffee trade at the dawn of a very different world order when peace resumed. Under this regime, the market of the main consumer—the United States, drinker of 80 percent of the world's coffee at the time—was apportioned among the major producers, thus softening the blow of the loss of the European market.

For the United States, the IACA was a major break with established trade policy that generally favored free international markets. The United States entered into it to support friendly nations in its hemisphere, thereby securing their resistance to Axis overtures during this time of global war. While the agreement did not survive long after the war, it set an important precedent for U.S. engagement with Latin America and its coffee sector under the similar pressures of the Cold War. Furthermore, during the development of the IACA the U.S. government worked closely with the large domestic coffee roasters, a relationship that would prove to be quite enduring.

Following the war, under the aggressive economic reconstruction of the Marshall Plan, European demand recovered quite rapidly. Producing stocks in both Brazil and Colombia, however, had declined, and prices quadrupled by 1950. Both countries had liquidated their surpluses during the war, and in the midst of this rising demand and limited stocks a severe frost in Brazil in 1953 sent prices skyrocketing.

Geopolitically, the United States was confirmed as the hegemonic power in the region and remained the world's dominant consumer of coffee. Consequently, in the years immediately following the war, the United States was the biggest opponent of cartelization of the world coffee market. Postwar

This 1960s ad for Portuguese colonial coffee replaces brutal forced labor with erotic exoticism—quite a stretch.

Green Coffee Exports

Source: FAO

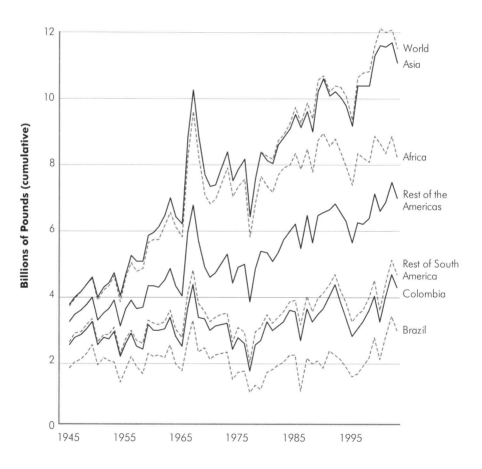

coffee-price increases caused the United States to reinstitute domestic price controls that had been lifted at the conclusion of the war. This put the United States in direct economic opposition to both the producing nations and its own coffee roasting industry. The "five-cent cup of coffee" had become a potent symbol of prosperity in the postwar United States, and coffee prices had acquired a symbolism that went beyond strictly economic terms.

As the gap between the price set by the producers and the price taken by the United States grew, a black market in coffee developed that obliged the U.S. government to subsidize roasters and traders in order to make legally traded coffee available at the mandated price. This untenable situation reached its apogee at a series of Senate subcommittee hearings in 1949 and 1950 about coffee prices, during which heartland senators sought to cast themselves as the defenders of the U.S. consumer against the unfair practices of foreign cartels (predictably, these hearings got much more press in Brazil than in the United States, as had similar hearings around the time of valorization).

Climbing prices in the 1940s and especially the 1950s led to a wave of new plantings around the world. In Brazil, important new centers of coffee production emerged, and an African coffee industry based on robustas began to assert itself in the international market as European colonial powers sought to develop export crops for their colonies.

In addition to its use in instant coffee, robusta also became a lower-priced substitute for expensive arabicas. In the 1950s it started to appear in roast ground coffee for consumer use—first in Europe, where its use was promoted in countries with robusta-producing colonies such as France (French West Africa) and Portugal (Angola), then in the United States.

During the early 1950s planners in Brazil and Colombia foresaw a predictable replay of the same old coffee cycle. Both countries had embraced coffee as the engine of development. Brazil in particular was using the millions flowing into government coffers to fund massive projects, including the construction of Brazil's modern capital, Brasilia. In 1953 these nations resolved to take advantage of the high prices to come to a renewed collusive arrangement that would forestall the otherwise inevitable period of stagnation.

In 1954 an FNC delegation to Brazil (in which the managing director had achieved the rank of ambassador) came to an agreement over Colombian and Brazilian production. In 1957 Brazil and Colombia managed to obtain the cooperation of other Latin American producers, thus forming a cartel that established export limits for all Latin American coffee producers.

Unfortunately for both Brazil and Colombia, they faced a replay of the damaging failure of the 1936 scheme. African producers, who were outside the cartel, continued to increase production. Central American producers, while fulfilling their quotas, incurred no costs in participating and became free riders. Meanwhile, the governments of both Brazil and Colombia ran budget deficits buying their own producers' coffee in order to keep it off the market. Brazil quickly accumulated stocks equal to half the global annual coffee consumption. By 1959 Brazilian stocks nearly equaled total world exports.

Worse, unlike 1937, the large producers were unable to retaliate against the free riders and outsiders. They would have suffered the most from dumping their excess supply onto the world market. Finally, the FNC developed a new plan: the cartel could be enforced by consumers.

In the world of coffee, particularly in the 1950s, "consumers" meant the United States, which bought 58 percent of the coffee exported globally in that decade. The challenge facing Colombia and Brazil, then, was to bring the United States into their scheme. Essentially, they hoped to have the world's largest consumer of coffee enforce a pact whereby that consumer paid more for coffee than under an open regime.

Difficult as this sounds, it was made even less likely at that time because the United States had been going through a period of antipathy toward international commodity agreements that impeded free markets. To make matters worse, in the case of coffee, the U.S. consumer had been enjoying the falling prices after the 1953 price jump.

Fortunately for the Latin American regimes, in the 1940s and 1950s the United States was developing a policy of hegemonic exclusion of Communist influence from Latin America. Domestically, obsessive fear of Communism in Latin America made it possible to contemplate price-setting cartels in the interest of supporting non communist regimes.

In 1958, the Eisenhower administration directed the Department of State to organize a Coffee Study Group with the National Coffee Association, the roasters' lobbying organ, to investigate the situation. The United States seemed willing to spend any amount to assure itself that these (and all other) countries were immune to the charms of Communism. It established a series of outreach initiatives—including the Organization of American States—with the goal of staving off Communism through more and closer links with the United States.

International development also became an important focus in the foreign affairs of developed nations, and new organizations such as the United Nations developed major agendas aimed at improving the worldwide standard of living. Unfortunately for the citizens of many of these less-developed nations (famously dubbed the "Third World" by French demographer Alfred Sauvy in 1952), these good intentions were quickly caught up in the politics of the Cold War.

Aid money, much of it military, became a reward system for the corrupt client regimes of the superpower antagonists. Development usually took the form of showcase engineering projects such as dams, power plants, and railroads. In an era of unquestioned faith in technology, such infrastructure along with industrialized Green Revolution agricultural schemes swept aside thousands of years of locally developed

The National Coffee Association (NCA)

Formed in 1911 in St. Louis as an emergency measure to loan coffee to Mississippi Delta roasters whose supply had been cut off by an outbreak of yellow fever in New Orleans, the National Coffee Association (so named in 1940) quickly became a permanent, national presence representing roasters and importers throughout the United States.

One of the oldest U.S. trade associations, the NCA provides expertise, lobbying coordination, generic coffee consumption promotion, and information dissemination for the industry. It has also funded extensive research into the health effects of coffee drinking, particularly in the 1970s and 1980s when coffee had been implicated in a number of health problems.

Now located in New York City, in a building near the site of the old Merchant's Coffeehouse, the NCA publishes the annual National Coffee Drinking Trends Report and holds an annual convention at

systems and knowledge, all with very little real improvement in the lives of most people living in developing countries.

Crops like coffee were seen by many as a first step toward development. By attracting foreign exchange, export crops inject money into national economies that would, it was hoped, stimulate the generalized improvement of the standard of living. How this was to work in entrenched systems that had been set up by colonial plantation owners in order to effect the exact opposite was never clear.

In fact, subsequent history has shown that coffee as a development tool works best when its production is decentralized and involves many smallholders rather than a few large producers. When organized this way, coffee is better at bringing capital into less-developed nations than many other primary commodities, including tea, sugar, cocoa, bananas, oranges, cotton, and tobacco. It also tends to be more redistributive—spreading the money it brings in to more people in the producing country—than mineral commodities such as petroleum and bauxite (aluminum ore). Even so, only one country—Brazil—can truly be said to have initiated successful development with coffee. As the world's largest producer by far (currently over 30 percent of world production, and as much as 80 percent during key stages of its development push), Brazil's situation was very different than that of any other would-be coffee power.

As the Cold War progressed, U.S. policy priorities continued to shift away from the five-cent cup of coffee toward the stabilization of noncommunist regimes in Latin America. In 1962, with extreme oversupply causing ever-falling coffee prices (stocks were well on their way to totaling double annual consumption), many analysts were convinced that the Latin American economies were on the verge of collapse and warned of the potential political consequences. The Brazilian economy in particular, 51 percent of which came from coffee earnings, was seen as the keystone in maintaining U.S. influence in the region.

By 1963, at the time of the Cuban Missile Crisis, the shift was nearly complete. John F. Kennedy's Alliance for Progress—a massive capital infusion into Latin America for the explicit purpose of thwarting Communism in the region—was seriously threatened by an open coffee market. As Kennedy noted, "a drop of one cent a pound for . . . coffee costs Latin American producers $50 million in export proceeds—enough to seriously undercut what we are seeking to accomplish by the Alliance for Progress."[1] Other commentators were even more blatant. The ostensibly liberal senator Hubert Humphrey, for example, claimed in 1963, "[Raising coffee prices] is a matter of life or death, a matter of Castroism versus freedom . . . Castroism will spread like the plague through Latin America unless something is done about the prices of the raw materials produced there; and those prices can be stabilized on an international basis."[2]

By this time, the Latin American regimes had become adept at playing the United States for economic benefit. Handsomely supported as clients of U.S. foreign policy, they certainly knew how to pull the strings of their Uncle Sam.

which the state of the nation's industrial coffee industry is gauged.

The NCA remains a bastion of the industrialized, commodified coffee industry; the growing specialty coffee industry is represented by its own trade group, the Long Beach–based Specialty Coffee Association of America (SCAA).

Colombian senator Enrique Escovar put it bluntly: "Pay us good prices for our coffee or—God help us all—the masses will become one great Marxist revolutionary army that will sweep us all into the sea."[3]

Contemporary materials from the Pan-American Coffee Bureau, the Latin American producers' lobbying group in the United States, declared, "Every time an American lifts a cup of coffee to his lips, he symbolically affects the welfare of some 20,000,000 persons around the world whose livelihood depends on coffee. In Latin America alone, some 13,000,000 people are dependent on the economic health of coffee. . . . Total U.S. economic assistance to the 15 Latin American coffee countries in the first full year under the Alliance for Progress program . . . amounted to $707.5 million. Yet, during the same period, those countries lost $640 million due to the drop in coffee prices."[4]

The stage was set; the new, improved International Coffee Agreement proposed by Brazil and Colombia was ready to be instituted. One final factor made it a reality: the corporations who stood to profit the most.

The Corporations and the Communist Threat

In the 1950s the U.S. coffee market was, like most other sectors of the economy, undergoing a period of conglomeration. In the coffee sector this meant that roasters, and especially roasting capacity, were being concentrated in the hands of a few major corporations as regional roasters such as Folgers, Hills Brothers, and Maxwell House were absorbed by them.

General Foods, through its Maxwell House and other brands, controlled 15 percent of world coffee consumption in 1965. This accounted for half of the corporation's profit that year, and invested buyers' trips to producing countries with the import of a state visit. During this time, National Coffee Association (NCA) members collectively represented almost 45 percent of global consumption.

Coffee consumption in the United States was at its peak in the 1950s and 1960s. The huge roasters' main interest was in maintaining a profitable relationship with consumers, and stable prices could help them do that. Free market price lows did little to increase any individual roaster's market share, while price highs generated by the same coffee cycle simply drove away consumers to competing beverages, such as tea and, for the first time, soft drinks.

When the International Coffee Agreement (ICA) was under consideration in the early 1960s, the government used the same approach as it had with the wartime IACA: it called upon industry to guide its development. (Indeed, both those in government in favor of the agreement and those opposed sought counsel from the industry.) The U.S. delegation to the UN Coffee Conference in 1962 consisted of eleven government officials and eight representatives of the NCA.

Nevertheless, the industry downplayed any financial benefit that might have accrued to it, and instead emphasized the importance of fighting Communism. George Robbins, at that time the Director of Green Coffee Operations for General Foods (GF), and "undoubtedly, the single most important business figure in determining the industry posture . . . [was,] according to a former Deputy Secretary of State, . . . 'a veritable coffee potentate,' and by most accounts, an executive quite willing to wield his company's enormous buying power—he personally purchased one seventh of the world's coffee—to get his way with coffee-reliant [countries]."[5] In Robbins' words:

> You would have had a crisis on your hands if this income [to Latin American countries] had been stopped. . . . Really it was quite simple. Politically, the countries would have been helpless. From a security standpoint of the United States, if Latin America had gone down the drain and the Communists taken over, they would have been right at our back door. And this would have been an uncomfortable and unhealthy situation for the United States.
>
> GF had a very small advantage, if any, to secure from the Coffee Agreement. With our tremendous buying power . . . we could always take advantage in situations of distress in one country or another. This can't be done now with the Coffee Agreement. The profits I used to turn in for GF were unbelievable—tremendous— many millions of dollars net every year. I didn't want to have my hands tied and yet I felt it was good for the solidarity and soundness of the world. A man has to decide sometimes where he stands with humanity.[6]

While it is inconceivable to think of the representative of a major corporation today speaking in such terms, there was more at stake for General Foods than just the "solidarity and soundness of the world."

In retrospect, 1962 was the golden age of corporate coffee in the United States, and the roasters certainly had little to fear—or thought they had little to fear—from higher prices, especially if they were coupled with guaranteed supplies that could help them lock in their market dominance. Coffee is an addictive stimulant, after all, and consumers would happily pay more. Coffee seemed impervious to normal market forces.

But even market maturity does not explain the relentless and deeply involved nature of the roasters' advocacy. The Eisenhower-era Coffee Study Group, for example, which represented the first time U.S. participation in an international coffee cartel had been publicly contemplated, was the result of a quiet program of lobbying by GF and other giant U.S. roasters that reached back well before that coffee heyday. It seems that another force was in play.

The large roasters, because of the structure of their trading relationships with the large producers, were to a great extent beholden to Brazil and Colombia for their continued market domination. While the sword cuts both ways, it was clear that in the early 1960s the large roasters in the United States were expected by their suppliers at the FNC and the Instituto to promote the ICA within the United States. To do otherwise would have risked their lucrative and massive contracts with the producers. Robert Bates, a former member of the U.S. delegation to the International Coffee Organization, recounts an exchange he had on this subject with the head of Folgers:

> Procter and Gamble, the second largest roaster of coffee in the United States, cultivates a reputation for a strong commitment to "all-American" values: patriotism, capitalism and competitive markets. In a telephone interview, I once questioned the head of its coffee division about the agreement, and he indicated that he did not support it and that "the free market would be OK." "We may in fact testify in Congress against it," he added. "How about Brazilian reprisals?" I asked. "Would they be likely to punish you by canceling your contracts?" There was a long pause before the executive replied, "Don't even breathe that possibility to anyone else. I will have to explain to our Chief Executive that the Brazilians may force us on board. I would be less than honest if I didn't say this to him. The Brazilians price coffee so attractively to us— we go with that contract and buy big and use it. We buy all we can get. But then they can put the screws on us."[7]

Furthermore, these large corporations are transnationals, and many had other investments in the producer countries. A 1967 dispute with Brazil over that country's exports of instant coffee forced both Brazil and the roasters to show their hands. During this tense period the continuation of any international coffee agreement was at stake, and passions were running high. Brazil managed to force Coca-Cola (the owner of Tenco, an instant coffee company[8]) to back off from its original position opposing Brazilian actions by threatening to limit price increases on Coca-Cola in Brazil. Coca-Cola succumbed, even though Brazilian exports of cheap instant coffee had caused layoffs at Tenco's New Jersey plant.

(This incident was also important because it demonstrated the limitations of the U.S. government's commitment to development in the Latin American countries, or at least the limitations of its ability to act on its commitment. While the establishment of processing plants in Brazil moved more of the commodity chain within that country's borders and thus contributed more to that country's economy than the export of unprocessed green beans, it also put the Brazilian operation in direct competition with the U.S. food conglomerates. In this showdown the conglomerates proved to be the more important constituents of the U.S. administration, and the standoff ended when the Brazilians were forced to impose an export tax on their instant coffee.)

So, in 1962, at the behest of Colombia and Brazil and at the urging of the large U.S. roasters and the State Department, and in spite of any concerns over free trade or previously paramount low prices for the U.S. consumer, the International Coffee Agreement was born.

The International Coffee Organization (ICO) that emerged in 1963 to administer the ICA was a global cartel that assigned quotas to both producing and consuming countries. All trade in coffee between member countries was accompanied by permits, which were collected by the customs services of importing countries and sent on to the ICO offices in London.

The ICO aimed to control supply through quotas, which were adjusted to maintain an agreed-upon price spread between different coffee grades. Producing countries met quota obligations by stockpiling coffee to keep it off the market, destroying it, or selling it at low prices to non-ICO countries, principally Soviet-bloc and developing nations.

Voting power in the ICO was derived from market share, institutionalizing the dominance of Brazil, Colombia, and the United States. Suddenly the international trade in coffee was a very different game. The politics of coffee commerce moved into the back rooms of the ICO, and its annual meeting became a spectacle of politicking, influence peddling, and intimidation in which producers and consumers jockeyed for their interests in discussions over the setting of quotas and indicator prices for different grades of coffee.

An additional layer of politics was embedded in the system because the ICA had to be renegotiated every five years. At these meetings, the glad-handing and back-stabbing reached a fever pitch, and several times during the history of the ICA it was allowed to lapse when agreement was impossible. Still, as long as there was a commitment by the three parents of the agreement, the system continued to function.

With the participation of the consuming countries, the ICA was far more effective at regulating the trade in coffee than any of its forerunners. During its reign coffee prices remained relatively stable and relatively high. Coffee production came to be seen as a viable means of development for tropical countries that had not produced it before or had done so only in limited quantities. Central American and African nations, and Indonesia in particular, undertook massive expansions of their coffee industries, often with the assistance and encouragement of the World Bank and the

International Monetary Fund (IMF). However, because these countries were either outside the ICA or had a limited quota allotment within it, much of this added production could only be sold at low (though stable) prices to countries outside the ICA. Throughout the 1970s this trend went unchecked. Planted acreage increased dramatically, often with modern, high-yielding strains of coffee that could grow without shade.

The ICA had the effect of further concentrating the coffee roasting industry, as it made coffee more expensive for small roasters in consuming countries. This tendency had been foreseen by the smaller sectors of the industry, but even by 1962 they were able to do little more than complain:

> The monstrous International Coffee Cartel set up with the support of our Government, contrary to our Trust Busting laws, is having the only effect it can have. The big are getting bigger and the small have the hangman's noose around the neck tightening daily. Some have retired voluntarily, and others involuntarily. . . . Suddenly free men, with traditions of Boston Tea Parties, have lost their tongues, mesmerized by the soft tones of Washington politicians.[9]

At the same time, the development goals of the ICA, which included "the promotion and maintenance of employment and income in the member countries, thereby helping to bring about fair wages, higher living standards, and better working conditions,"[10] were never really acted upon. The diversification fund it established to facilitate a switch to other crops was never sufficient to accomplish very much, which is perhaps a good thing, given its track record by 1972:

> All too often "other crops" is beef cattle grazing, as old coffee soil is virtually useless for anything else, and grazing requires minimal labour compared with coffee which

is a labour-intensive crop. Fair wages is a meaningless phrase to the often starving migrant workers in Latin America, to the thousands who leave the huge plantations all over Latin America to crowd into the overcrowded shanty towns on the peripheries of the large cities. All the grand notions of "fair wages, higher living standards, and better working conditions" are nothing more than words when black workers on Portuguese-owned plantations in Angola work with guns at their backs. None of these words will be realized until there is massive land reform throughout the producing countries, but the United States, the most influential importing Member of the ICO, has done its utmost in the past to prevent any such land reform from taking place in Latin America. The large landowners of Africa and Latin America who try to block land reform programmes irrespective of their radical or mildly reformist nature are precisely the owners of the large coffee plantations.[11]

If the ICA served to prolong the golden moment when huge producers and huge roasters stood shoulder-to-shoulder in the warm glow of virtuous anticommunist prosperity, by the 1980s this ossified arrangement was showing new strains as the world order fundamentally changed around it.

Changes in coffee production had created a vast global surplus concentrated in countries that had not heretofore been coffee powers. As long as the quota system barred their rising output from access to lucrative ICA markets, countries like Costa Rica grumbled about having to barter their high-quality beans at half the ICA price for vehicles and power stations from cash-strapped non–ICA Eastern European countries.

Changes in consumer preference for brewed over instant coffee (and thus for arabicas over robustas) were not met by changes in supply due to the political rather than market nature of allocation. Indeed, much of the high-quality coffee from newer producers was available only in Eastern Europe, in countries outside the ICA. This alienated major U.S. roasters. They became downright frightened in 1985 when the European food products firm Nestlé entered the U.S. market in roast coffee through its purchase of Hills Brothers (from the investment firm that had come to own the brand) as well as independent holdouts Chase & Sanborn and MJB. Because Nestlé was based in Europe and had roasting facilities in Berlin, U.S. roasters feared that it might gain access to cheap non-ICA member coffee from Eastern Europe.

The U.S. Department of State had by the 1980s shifted its focus in Latin America away from South America and toward its "near abroad"—Mexico and Central America. Nevertheless, the rigid structure of the ICA made it impossible for the United States to use the coffee trade to reward friendly governments in this region. Support from the U.S. foreign-policy establishment thus also waned, leaving the ICA without a crucial leg.

The ICA was just one of many contemporary multilateral trade agreements covering everything from tin to olive oil. The ICA stood out, however, as the most complete and effective example, largely because of committed U.S. participation.[12] Nevertheless, the ICA was not immune to changing political tides: as renewed enthusiasm for free markets and diminished interest in development swept the industrialized world, very few of these agreements survived the 1980s. Toward the end of the decade, the Reagan administration in the United States decided to sabotage ICA renewal negotiations by making politically untenable demands of Brazil and Colombia (specifically, that they increase the quotas of washed arabicas from Central America) and by packing the U.S. delegation with University of Chicago economists—famously adamant free-marketeers.

The ICA had been abandoned by its pillars of support: the roasters, the U.S. government, and the small producers. At the renewal negotiations of 1989, only the old diehards, Brazil and Colombia, remained committed to it. The ICO lost its power to set and enforce export and import quotas, and in its 1994 renegotiation it became merely an international information dissemination and promotional trade group, no longer even including the United States among its members. (At the NCA's behest, the United States rejoined the eviscerated body in 2005, with Secretary of State Condoleezza Rice citing "impressive reforms.")

Today's Traded Bean

The functional collapse of the International Coffee Agreement in 1989 launched the modern era in the world of coffee. Prices plummeted immediately, and stayed at historic lows for five years. During this time, real prices fell to levels heretofore unseen in the twentieth century. In the producing countries, the party was over. In countries that derived a major part of their receipts from the export of coffee—over 70 percent for some Central African states—the damage to the national economy was devastating. In many cases, gross national product (GNP) was halved or worse in one crushing blow. Coffee-dependent economies all over the world saw their incomes drop by billions in a few short months.

In Brazil this crash was the final insult to an already teetering sector. Brazil had entered the century as *the* coffee economy. Coffee had been the spark that ignited the country's foreign trade and initiated the development of a modern economy. By 1989, coffee had fallen to a mere 5 percent of the nation's exports by value—less than 1 percent of GNP—as, throughout the century, coffee production had remained relatively constant while other sectors grew. With the collapse of the international market and renewed political change within the country, the storied Instituto fractured into war-

Green Coffee Imports

Source: FAO

ring factions, and Brazil's coffee sector degenerated into a disorganized system of smaller exporters.

With the demise of the ICA, the free market took over, but it did so in an environment that had become bloated from a quarter century of high, cartelized prices. Industries born under this relatively safe regime in Africa and Asia suffered terribly; worldwide, annual export earnings of coffee-producing countries dropped by $5 billion. Even in Brazil, the original master at playing coffee hardball, the old coffee cycle seemed to be back: trees were uprooted and land converted to other uses.

All over the world, the coffee trade was thrown into disarray as different actors struggled to find their places in the new coffee order. Coffee flooded onto the market as producers (who should have known better) panicked and liquidated their reserves. Prices plunged to their lowest levels since the Depression, and roasters and traders took advantage of the chaos to build up their supplies. Massive quantities of coffee were transferred from producers to consuming multinationals, who stockpiled furiously, giving them far greater leverage over sellers in subsequent years.

In Colombia the FNC stepped in to protect its members, running deficits for several years to offer a guaranteed minimum price for their crop and rebuilding a domestic stockpile. The FNC emerged from this period at last victorious over its old rival, Brazil. By the early 1990s Colombia was exporting nearly as much coffee as Brazil and getting a better price for it. Around the world, the FNC's advertising campaigns (relentless for more than a half century) had embedded, via Juan Valdez, the idea of Colombia as coffee and vice versa in the minds of consumers. But even this triumph was short-lived, as a new challenge shook the coffee world: the surprise emergence of Vietnam as a coffee power.

Although coffee has been grown in Vietnam since French colonial days and has been drunk there for a century (rare for Southeast Asia), the nation had not been a major producer. In the 1980s, however, new robusta plantations were established in the province of Dak Lak to supply Soviet-bloc instant coffee markets, and not incidentally to bring ethnic Vietnamese settlers to the restive wilderness near the Cambodian border.

But just as Vietnam's coffee investments were beginning to bear fruit, the simultaneous demise of the ICA and the Soviet Union allowed Vietnamese coffee to enter valuable Western markets, where it competed directly with coffee from established sources. As well, Vietnam suddenly had access to Western development investment. Money flooded into the country, first from France, but then also from the American-controlled IMF and World Bank.

Though the World Bank, which did not resume loans to Vietnam until 1994, officially insists that it did not directly finance coffee expansion, its infrastructure and capacity-building loans undoubtedly set the stage for government-sponsored efforts in this area, as well as joint ventures with transnationals like Nestlé. In 1999, five years after World Bank loans to Vietnam resumed, the country saw its largest increase by far in coffee area harvested as new plantings came on line. Two years later, as prices were hitting rock bottom, one of the bank's principal economists was quoted in the *San Francisco Chronicle* as saying "Vietnam has become a successful producer. In general, we consider it to be a huge success."[13]

Expanded market access and increased investment, plus a commitment to coffee from an authoritarian government, all combined with cheap labor, plenty of land, and a weak currency to rocket Vietnam from the middle of the pack of coffee producers in the mid-1980s to number two in 1999, a position it has held ever since. At the same time, an uncontrolled flood of farmers to the southern highlands, reminiscent of Colombia's coffee rush almost a century earlier, led to serious environmental degradation. Hundreds of thousands of acres of forestland were cut and burned, often illegally. In one 1997 case, local authorities found that almost 2,500 acres of forest had been cleared for unauthorized coffee planting in Dak Lak using funds that had been

Vietnamese Coffee Production

Source: FAO

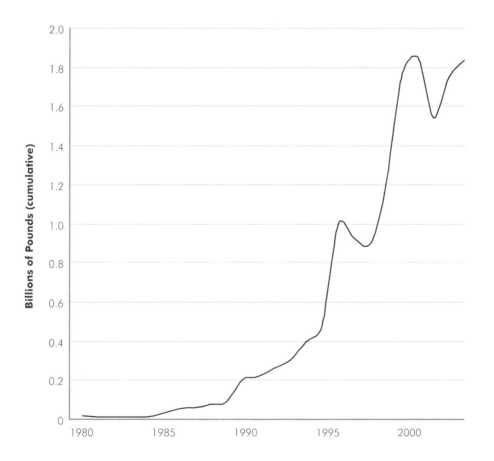

earmarked for reforestation. Additionally, coffee plantings transformed local water-sheds. Water supplies were diverted to thirsty coffee plants and wells drilled into the water table throughout the region. Subsequent water shortages during dry periods contributed to political unrest in the years to come.

Vietnamese coffee was technified right from the start, both on the lands of the small farmers responsible for 80 percent of the country's coffee, as well as on those owned directly by the Communist state. Though yields are among the highest in the world, vigorous technification combined with shoddy handling during processing and transport made Vietnamese coffee's quality consistently abysmal. At its worst, Vietnamese coffee could include moldy, immature beans inadequately dried over a fire of burning tires. Much of these beans were destined for regionally-consumed instant coffee or low-grade canned coffee for the Japanese market, though their abundance and cheapness quickly made them attractive to mass-market roasters around the world, lowering the bar for all producers.

The emergence of Vietnam could not have come at a worse time for established producers. By 1993, world coffee prices adjusted for inflation were at the same levels they had been during the Depression, when Brazil's Instituto do Café had been forced to "defend" coffee by destroying millions of bags. Compounding producers' woes was a continued antipathy toward any sort of state intervention in coffee markets on the part of American policymakers. Not only had the ICA been gutted but, as a result of structural adjustment requirements imposed by institutions like the World Bank and the IMF during the 1990s, national coffee boards from Indonesia to Côte d'Ivoire to Mexico to Kenya and beyond were all disbanded or rendered toothless. Even the Instituto do Café ceased operations after a century of coordinating and enforcing Brazilian coffee policy. While these bodies had been far from perfect representatives of farmers' interests—at times just the opposite—on balance they did serve to shelter small producers somewhat from the full fury of international commodity markets.

At the same time, the World Bank and IMF were vociferously insisting that indebted developing nations service their debts by producing export crops. With so many of the coffee-producing nations in the same straits, these demands only worsened the worldwide glut, driving countries deeper into debt they were even less able to pay. Prices quickly fell below costs for producers in many countries, and inputs and acreage decreased significantly—in 1993 alone, more than 800 million coffee trees were uprooted in Brazil, a free-market consequence of low prices that would have been resisted had the Instituto still been in place.

But when the slump came to an end, the result was only further chaos. In 1994, reports of multiple frosts in Brazil sent July coffee prices shooting to three times their levels at the start of the year. Was the old coffee cycle back? As usual, high prices prompted remaining producers to invest in their estates once more (though many had stagnated permanently during the slump due to lack of care), and new actors to enter the fray. But without the attenuating efforts of government coffee boards or international cooperation, the effects were even more extreme than usual.

In Vietnam, 300,000 acres of forestland in the central highlands were cleared and burned to make way for new coffee plantings. Freed of the constraints formerly imposed by the Instituto, new plantings in Brazil shifted the country further toward highly mechanized robusta production. New techniques like pivot irrigation and automated harvesting reduced labor inputs and consequently production costs on these plantations to some of the lowest ever seen—by one estimate, it would take a hundred workers harvesting traditional farms by hand to equal the output of one person on these new capital-intensive, hyper-technified farms.

The Coffee Crisis

By 1999, increased production led prices to fall even below the lows of the first part of the decade. In addition to Vietnam, production in India and Uganda had increased more than 30 percent through the 1990s, and Guatemala's and Ethiopia's production increased 20 to 25 percent. Brazil's bumper crop in 1998–99 also contributed significantly to oversupply.

In this perverse and disorganized world coffee market, production continued to rise even as prices fell, and the first few years of the millennium saw 2 billion more pounds of coffee produced annually than were consumed. The benchmark "C" Price did not rise above a dollar a pound for the next six years, when poor weather hit both Brazil and Vietnam. Adjusted for inflation, the 2001 low of 42 cents per pound may have been the lowest world price ever in coffee's thousand-year history of international trade. In Sumatra, a pound of coffee was worth less than a pound of rice at this time.

The Coffee Crisis, as this collapse became known, quietly shook the world. Families around the globe were forced from the land, crowding already overburdened tropical cities. National economies contracted sharply as coffee receipts fell by 75 percent from the peak in the mid-nineties. Even in low-cost Vietnam coffee prices covered only 60 percent of production costs.

Simultaneously, many countries were additionally hurt by a global economic downturn, a reduction in aid from developed countries, poor prices for other commodities, and, in some cases, hurricanes and droughts. Though dispersed and under the radar of developed-nation consumers (it received virtually no coverage by mainstream American media before 2002), the Coffee Crisis was a full-blown global development disaster. It probably directly affected 100 million people who earned their livelihoods from coffee, plus hundreds of millions more as national economies faltered.

Around the world, most families in coffee-growing regions could no longer afford to send their children to school or to buy basic medicines. Even food became hard to come by in some areas as destitute farmers, unable to pay their debts, forfeited their land. Almost half a million coffee pickers in Central America alone lost jobs that had been difficult and ill-paid ($3 per day or less) in the best of times. In places like Nicaragua, where nearly half of rural jobs are in coffee, the way of life in the countryside was completely disrupted.

Malnutrition broke out in places that had not seen it in a generation or more. Throughout Central America, 1.5 million people weren't able to get enough to eat, with an additional 8.6 million suffering less severe food insecurity. In 2003, 70 percent of children in Guatemala's coffee-growing regions were malnourished. In the same year, a third of the entire population of Nicaragua was malnourished, and a fifth of the nation's children were experiencing stunted growth as a result. Desperate coffee farmers marched on the capital, demanding help. Hundreds of thousands became undocumented migrants to neighboring Costa Rica or farther afield.

Even once-proud coffee nations like Colombia were brought to their knees, unable to pay their debt obligations or support social services for their citizens. In many ways, Colombia was the quintessential twentieth-century developing nation. Having passed through a series of boom-and-bust cycles, political turmoil, and Cold War hegemony, by the 1990s the nation was desperately trying to enter the world stage as a free-market democracy.

Colombia's major exports are all primary products that serve the needs of developed countries: fossil fuels (33 percent by value) and agricultural products like coffee (6 percent), cut flowers (4 percent), and illegal drugs (probably 3 or 4 percent) together

Most Coffee-Dependent Countries

Source: FAO, WTO, CIA

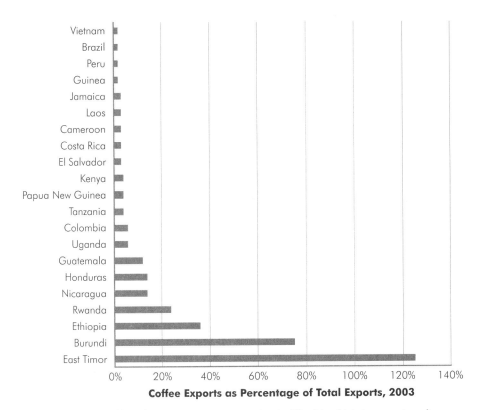

Coffee Exports as Percentage of Total Exports, 2003

Note: Accurate statistics are notoriously difficult to obtain in many struggling countries, as seen here in the case of East Timor

make up about half of the nation's exports. Most of the rest is accounted for by light manufacturing, especially of clothing, also in the service of developed countries. In the midst of grave political instability and violence throughout the twentieth century, Colombia's coffee-producing areas were a stable and calm beacon due to their historically more equitable income distribution and higher levels of development—a direct result of FNC work.

But chronically low prices forced the FNC to cut back its services, starting with price supports in the early nineties. Next went agronomic and development assistance to farmers. Neglect of the nation's technified plantations led to massive outbreaks of *la broca* and coffee rust. Unable to afford the pesticides they relied upon, farmers could only stand by and watch their crops fail. During this period, the FNC was even selling off its banking and shipping interests in a bid to remain in business. Even the long-standing advertising campaigns that had set Colombian coffee apart in the minds of coffee drinkers around the planet were not immune. In 2001, the actor who played Juan Valdez retired, and the FNC's storied meta-brand began to sink into the faceless brown seas of commodity coffee. Though Juan Valdez reappears from time to time to promote Colombian coffee, the FNC is struggling, desperate to market its way out of much more serious structural problems.

In their weakened state, Colombia's coffee-growing areas have been pulled into the country's festering civil war as dispossessed farmers have swelled the ranks of guerrilla armies (a step toward fulfilling Enrique Escovar's prophetic warning to American lawmakers almost fifty years earlier). As elsewhere in the Andes, low coffee prices have made other addictive tropical drugs also favored by rich-nation consumers much more attractive to farmers: many farmers have turned to coca and opium poppies, undermining crop-substitution efforts by the U.S. government.

Worldwide, the regime of careless capitalism contributed to one national tragedy after another. In the early 1990s, low coffee prices eviscerated Rwanda's economy.

Value of World Green Coffee Exports

Source: FAO

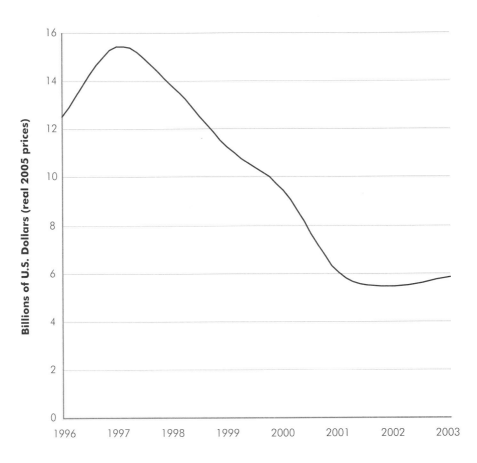

Eighty percent of the nation's export earnings had been from coffee, with the overwhelming majority of citizens growing at least some of the crop. This economic body blow combined with political instability and World Bank structural adjustment demands (which included an end to the Equalization Fund with which the government bought coffee from growers, an end to agricultural supports, and currency devaluation) helped push the country over the brink into the bloody meltdown of 1994. Half a million people were slaughtered and a quarter of the population became refugees.

Similarly, the 1994 Zapatista rebellion in Mexico included many coffee farmers, for whom low prices were the final indignity in decades of neglect enlivened by periodic exploitation. Indigenous farmers in the poorest parts of the country produced 60 percent of Mexico's coffee. In 2002, at the height of the Coffee Crisis, these farmers were only able to earn back about a third of the dollar it cost them to produce a pound of high-quality green arabica. A fifth of the harvest was left to rot on the trees.

By 2000, Vietnam's 600,000 small farmers had become trapped in the familiar cycle of debt as well, a microcosm of the situation for producing countries as a whole. The boomtime loans they had received to set up and operate their farms depended on continued high prices for their repayment and could no longer be serviced. The price crisis, combined with a drought caused by destruction and overexploitation of local watersheds for coffee production, provoked ethnic violence between minority groups and coffee settlers in Dak Lak. The army took two weeks to quell the strife, prompting the government to cut back for the first time on its support for new plantings. By 2001 the government was undertaking efforts to improve quality and had even announced plans to destroy hundreds of thousands of acres of coffee; still, the area harvested continued to increase thereafter, albeit more slowly.

The Coffee Crisis signaled not just a particularly bad swing in the long-standing coffee cycle, but a new structure for the global coffee trade, one in which life on the farm had reverted to a form that was palpably reminiscent of coffee's days of overt slavery on colonial plantations. It's not surprising that the desperation unleashed by the crisis eventually made it back to consuming nations: in one well-known 2001 case, six of the fourteen illegal immigrants to the United States who died of exposure in the Arizona desert were found to be destitute small-scale coffee producers from Veracruz trying for a better life in a land where their coffee sells for twenty times what they could earn for it back home.

Worldwide, the financial impact of the crisis was equivalent to the United States, the world's biggest development donor, halving its aid budget.

The Bottom Line

Farmers weren't the only ones to suspect something was amiss in the way coffee was priced for consumers in the midst of growers' worst slump ever.

In 1990, high retail prices in the face of the lowest green coffee prices of the century raised the suspicion of consumer watchdogs, including the UK's Monopolies and Mergers Commission. This provided a rare, though limited, opportunity to see how the final stages of coffee's journey to your cup is affected, usually a very difficult proposition, as the economist John Talbot explains:

First, the largest players in these markets are huge diversified [transnational corporations], and it is almost impossible to sort out how much profit they make on their coffee operations as opposed to their other product lines. Second, information on costs of production can legally be considered a "trade secret," which does not have to be disclosed. The difficulty presented by this aspect of coffee manufacturing in the [consuming countries] is highlighted by the 1991 report of the United Kingdom Monopolies and Mergers Commission (MMC) on the prices of instant coffee. The MMC was asked to investigate Nestlé's pricing practices following the 1989 price crash, after which the retail prices of instant coffee generally remained at their pre-crash levels. In the United Kingdom, over 90 percent of the coffee consumed is in instant form, and in 1990, Nestlé brands accounted for 56 percent of the retail market. The MMC was asked to investigate whether Nestlé's position in the market allowed it to make monopoly profits following the price crash. But almost all of the data on Nestlé's profits are suppressed in the public version of the report, because it "would not be in the public interest to disclose [them]."[14]

Talbot estimates that Nestlé's profit was 25 percent on retail sales of its instant coffee in the United Kingdom between 1985 and 1989. The MMC report went on to find that no unfair anti-competitive activity had taken place, although Talbot notes:

What is considered to be [Nestlé's] competition in this analysis [of the British market in the late 1980s] is instructive: the second largest share in the market (25 percent) is held by General Foods Ltd., the Philip Morris/Kraft/General Foods United Kingdom subsidiary . . . all companies considered are large diversified [transnational corporations] who collectively benefit from their [overwhelming market dominance]; together they account for 95 percent of the market. Although there are no "anti-competitive" discussions of pricing policy among these firms, none are needed; they all know what the other firms are doing and respond accordingly. In this situation, Nestlé doesn't need to resort to "anti-competitive practices" and none of its [transnational] competitors are likely to complain about Nestlé's higher profits, as long as theirs are sufficient.[15]

When you buy a pound of coffee at your local supermarket, you are buying more than coffee. You are buying the packaging, the transportation, the roasting, the grading and sorting, the processing, and the picking that had to take place before you and the beans could meet up—a series of economic linkages between the producer and the user known as the value chain. Each link in the chain comprises a different phase of ownership, during which the product (coffee in this case) is transformed in some way.

For coffee, the generalized value chain consists of growing, primary processing, export, shipping, distribution, roasting, packaging, redistribution, brewing, and drinking. There can be more or fewer links in the chain depending on the specific circumstances of a given bean.

Most commodities are traded not only physically but as futures as well, and have specialized markets that coordinate this activity. In the case of coffee, the two most important global exchanges are the Coffee Terminal Market of London (robustas) and the Coffee, Sugar, and Cocoa Exchange of New York (arabicas). On these exchanges, participants can agree to a sale of coffee at a set price at a given time in the future. When the time arrives, that price is locked in, regardless of what is happening in the market.

In this way, large buyers can use the futures market to "hedge" their purchases. Hedging means taking a futures position opposite to their actual purchasing, so, no matter what happens in the market, they will both win and lose, and thereby obtain price stability.

Because the coffee supply can be so drastically altered by weather, the ability to

Supermarket Coffee Prices in the U.S.

Source: ICO, USDOL

Even as green coffee prices have gone down, prices for canned supermarket coffee have gone up. Green coffee is becoming a smaller and smaller part of the cost of what's in the can.

absorb future risk in this way is an important component of a smoothly running market. In July, during the Brazilian winter, coffee traders worldwide monitor the weather there much more closely than the weather in their own backyards. At the slightest hint or even rumor of a frost a frenzy of trading can erupt, sending traders scurrying around amid a frantic din of yelling and screaming.

Quickly buying contracts when it looks like coffee will be scarce in the future means, if such predictions are borne out, that the contracts can be resold later for many times their purchase price. Lucky traders in the mid-1970s, for example, saw their investments increase five times or more; of course, many have lost their money as well.

These jitters are made all the more volatile, and can be turned into price spikes, by the actions of speculators. These traders are in the market simply to make money from price changes and have no intention of ever taking delivery of a single bean. Speculators, which include huge commodities funds conducting computerized technical trading—trading based on patterns in market changes, rather than on realities on the coffee farm—have completely altered the coffee futures market. While it is still possible to use the market to hedge purchases—if you are holding a futures contract when it matures the coffee will, in fact, show up—by 1994 nine-tenths of coffee trading was purely speculative.

The result is increased market volatility as rumor ripples through the market and as large traders try to second-guess one another to make money on small price changes. All of this has virtually nothing to do with the people who have to try and put food on the table with the coffee they are growing, yet it determines the price they receive for their crop—and they don't have the luxury of hedging.

Aside from speculators, who add nothing and yet can make a lot of money, and growers, who produce the very coffee upon which the whole value chain is based and yet earn very little, most of the people making up the coffee value chain earn their living by adding value to the coffee in their control. The transformation may take the form of a physical change to the coffee (washing, roasting, grinding, and so on) or it may involve moving the coffee (by hand, by mule, by truck, by boat, by train). The amount of value that is added consists of the costs incurred to undertake the transformation at that link, plus some profit or surplus. This profit is, of course, the goal driving most of the actors in any value chain, and anyone involved with any value chain will tend to try and appropriate as much of it as they can.

In a free market, the money that enters a value chain all comes ultimately from the final consumer. For all of the other actors in the chain, yours is the only money coming in for that pound of beans, and they have to allocate it among themselves.

The way they do this is through a series of market interactions—buying and selling—at each level of the chain. The factors influencing these interactions include access to capital and information, political and regulatory structures, location, and weather. Basically, though, when you spend a dollar on coffee, part of that money stays with the retailer, who passes the rest on to the roaster through wholesale roast coffee purchases. The roaster in turn passes on some of your money to the green bean importers, who in turn pass less on to exporters in producing countries, who purchase from middlemen, who purchase from the farmers. The more links in the chain, the more dispersed your dollar becomes. If you buy a latte at a café, for example, part of your money goes to the café, part enters commodity value chains for milk, sugar, paper, and cinnamon, and part starts on its long journey toward the coffee grower.

One reason why coffee is such an important commodity to the global economy is that the value chain that moves coffee from less-developed nations into developed ones also moves money in the other direction; it is a major source of income for many of the poorest people in the poorest countries. This kind of foreign exchange is cru-

Coffee Trading System

Source: Talbot, 1997; Waridel, 1997

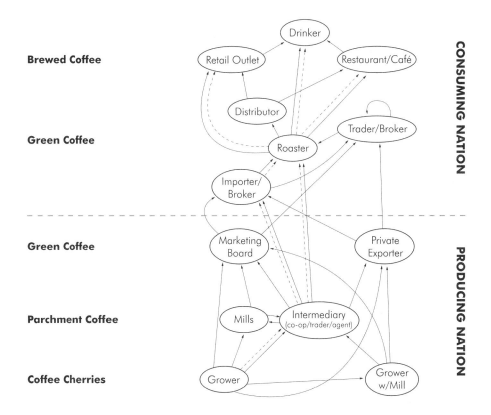

Coffee can travel a multitude of pathways from grower to drinker. Fair Trade relationships (dotted) eliminate many redundant linkages.

cial to poor countries if they hope to be able to buy the goods and services of the developed countries—products perceived as necessary for improving the standard of living of their citizens.

It follows that undertaking more than just the primary processing in the producing countries would further increase the amount of foreign exchange flowing into those countries. Moving more of the value chain into the producing countries—by roasting coffee and manufacturing instant coffee, for example—creates a potentially more powerful engine of development.

But this can be at odds with the goals of other parts of the chain. In the 1960s producing nations began to develop processing facilities (particularly instant coffee manufacturing plants) to capture more of the value chain within their borders. While much of this development took place with the help of certain transnationals (especially Nestlé, which has been particularly active in establishing processing facilities in major producing countries such as Brazil and Côte d'Ivoire), other transnationals preferred to have processing take place in consuming countries. During the reign of the International Coffee Agreement, the balance was tipped toward the producers with the cooperation of consuming-country governments who, for their own foreign policy reasons, sought to increase the income of coffee-producing countries.

Since the ICA collapsed in 1989, the result has been a shift of much of the value chain into the consuming countries—or, more precisely, into the transnationals based in consuming countries—thus reducing the income of producing countries further. In 1986, 37 cents of every dollar spent for retail roasted coffee in the United States flowed to developing countries. Fifteen years later, in 2001, only 12 cents made the trip all the way to producing countries, a reduction of 70 percent during a period when the retail price of coffee increased by more than 40 percent in real terms in the United States. In Japan, retail prices doubled during this period. Worse, the dismantling of coffee boards and export controls means that even that section of the value chain that takes place within a country's borders (and only 5 percent of coffee is processed beyond the green bean stage before leaving its country of origin) is not necessarily economically accessible—in many cases the only winners are the transnational corporations that control most of the middle part of the value chain.

Indeed, the brief 1994 coffee price spike was the perfect place to see the new order in operation. Brought on in part by frost in Brazil but exacerbated by speculative trading, this spike was less severe and shorter-lived than similar events in the past because of the more diverse (and glutted) worldwide producer picture. Thanks to the quick spread of information through the system, the absence of credible producer groups, and nimble maneuvering on the part of the roasters, virtually all of the price increase was captured by the transnational segment of the value chain.

Historically, proportionally more money had flowed to growers during times of high prices, such as after the 1975 Brazilian frosts. Under the new system, even the good times weren't so good any more for producers. And during periods of low prices, the growers find themselves squeezed hard, even while retail coffee prices change lit-

Laotian banknote featuring coffee pickers. In spite of the Coffee Crisis, impoverished countries still look to coffee to pick up some foreign exchange.

The Coffee Value Chain

Source: Talbot, 2004

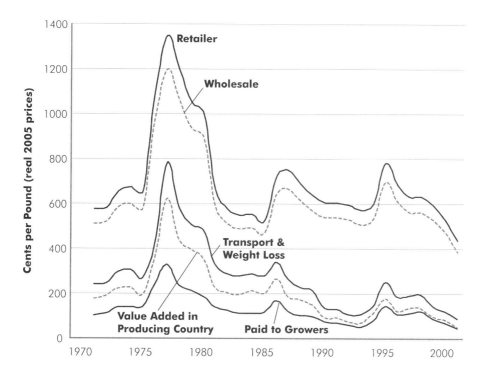

While the retail price of coffee has not changed all that much in the past fifteen years, transnational traders and roasters have captured an unprecedented slice of the value chain. In part, this has come from the efficiencies of containerization, but it has also come at the expense of growers and producing countries.

tle. Indeed, price spikes serve as convenient ways for roasters to raise retail prices—which rarely follow green coffee prices back down after a shock. This suggests that competition at the roasting level is lacking even though, in most developed nations, monopolies and collusion among major market actors are illegal, on the grounds that they distort the free market and keep profits (and thus consumer prices) unnaturally high. The economist John Talbot and other analysts estimate roaster profit on supermarket coffee to be around a quarter of the retail price, making it one of the best performers in the food and beverage sectors. No wonder coffee has been such a darling of these corporations.

Indeed, even during the height of the Coffee Crisis, while development agencies and coffee transnationals were publicly wringing their hands about the woes of coffee farmers worldwide, both were still actively taking steps to lower prices further. French development funds in Vietnam in 1998 paid for the expansion of nascent arabica production there, even as Nestlé was forcing other producers like Mexico to allow the importation of cheap Vietnamese robusta (Nestlé handles a quarter of Vietnam's exports, taking it to company-owned processing plants in other countries to blend into Nescafé). In 2002, while prices still hovered at historically low levels, the World Bank funded a project to promote coffee cultivation in Laos, and Nestlé was undertaking similar activity in Thailand and the Phillipines.

Perhaps the most astoundingly callous example of transnational bullying of coffee producers came in 2002, at the peak of the crisis. While 11 million people in Ethiopia were facing famine, Nestlé, with mediation by an arm of the World Bank, was demanding millions of dollars in compensation from that country for a company that had been nationalized by a previous government three decades earlier. After a public outcry in Europe that "shocked and surprised" Nestlé's CEO, the company said it would settle for $1.6 million, which it would magnanimously donate to famine relief.

Where a Coffee Dollar Goes

Source: Adopted from Talbot, *Tea & Coffee Journal*

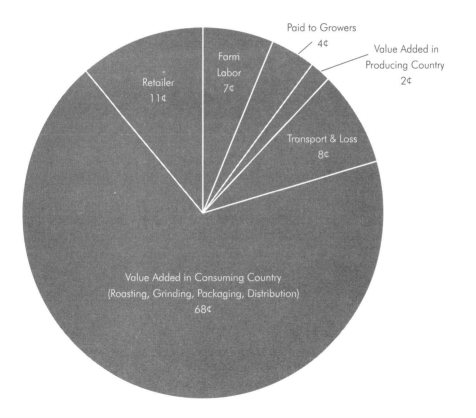

Paid to Growers
4¢

Value Added in
Producing Country
2¢

Farm
Labor
7¢

Retailer
11¢

Transport & Loss
8¢

Value Added in Consuming Country
(Roasting, Grinding, Packaging, Distribution)
68¢

In the post-1989 environment, the producers sought to revitalize their industry the only way they knew how—with another retention scheme. The 1993 Association of Coffee Producing Countries (ACPC), made up of Latin American and African producers representing 80 percent of world production, aimed to reduce exports by 20 percent. It was poorly organized, however, and, even in those countries that had the will, the capital to construct an effective regime was lacking. By 2001 even such lackluster efforts were abandoned by dejected producers. With producers played off one another by powerful transnationals who had by then absorbed the lion's share of the value chain, any collective power producers had in the past had been definitively smashed.

4

Health, Marketing, and the Mega-Roasters

The use of [coffee] will probably become greatly extended; as in other countries, it may diffuse itself among the mass of the people, and make a considerable ingredient in their daily sustenance.

—BENJAMIN MOSELEY, doctor and coffee enthusiast (1785)

Wired

CAFFEINE, THE FAMOUS ACTIVE INGREDIENT IN COFFEE, gives it that special edge. It makes coffee dangerous—habit-forming, stimulating, and sexy. Caffeine is the hidden half lurking behind the roasted aroma and luscious flavor of a good cup; together they create a compelling combination. And while coffee may be bad for the people and ecosystems that produce it, when taken in moderation it does not seem to cause undue harm to the human body.

Coffee contains several hundred chemicals, but its main physiologically active ingredient is technically known as 1,3,7-trimethylxanthine. Caffeine is one of a class of xanthine (pronounced "zantheen") compounds found in a long list of plant products, including tea leaves, cocoa beans, and coffee beans. Xanthines block the action of a neurotransmitter and neuromodulator named adenosine. By blocking the ability of adenosine to bind with its receptors in the brain and elsewhere (binding causes sedation), caffeine stimulates brain activity. Two cups of coffee are enough to stimulate brain arousal on an EEG (electroencephalograph), and higher doses (around four

Caffeine Concentrations

Source: *Buzzed*, The Coca–Cola Company, Erowid

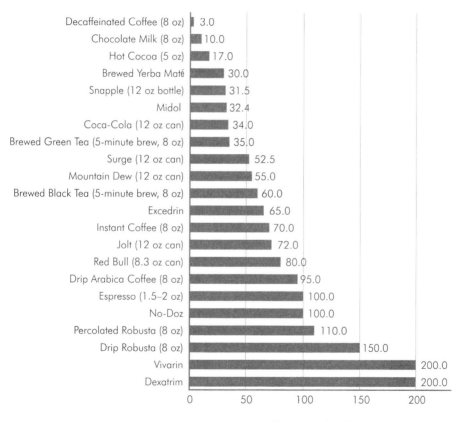

Milligrams of Caffeine

or five cups) increase heart rate and breathing. Most caffeine-tolerant java junkies, however, experience a reduced effect.

An average cup of joe contains about 80 to 150 milligrams of caffeine. For comparison, cola drinks contain about 30 to 50 milligrams per can. Although an ounce of tea leaves contains more caffeine than an ounce of ground coffee, an average cup of coffee has more caffeine because it takes more ground coffee to make a cup of java than it takes tea leaves to make a cup of tea. While espresso has a higher concentration of caffeine than regular coffee, the average serving is typically only 1.5 to 2 ounces—so the caffeine dose is about equal to that of a regular cup of coffee.

The type of coffee, the kind of roast, the level of grind, and the method of brewing all affect how much caffeine you drink with each cup. Robustas can have up to twice the amount of caffeine of finer specialty arabicas. Although they taste stronger, darker roasted beans actually have less caffeine than lighter roasts, as the longer roasting time breaks down more of it. Because of the larger surface area per unit volume, finer grinds increase the dose of caffeine extracted from the beans.

Within thirty to sixty minutes after ingestion, caffeine reaches peak levels in the body. Caffeine stimulates the sympathetic nervous system, which regulates our autonomic functions, such as breathing, heart rate, and digestion. As a central nervous system stimulant, it relieves fatigue and makes us feel more alert and able to think more quickly. Absorbed in the stomach and intestines, caffeine is eventually broken down by the liver, and its breakdown products are excreted through the kidneys. (Some caffeine is excreted too: municipal sewage treatment agencies report a midmorning surge of caffeine in America's wastewater.)

Too much coffee brings on "caffeinism," a condition characterized by anxiety, irritability, nervousness, lightheadedness, and even diarrhea. Caffeine dependence makes drinkers rely on a regular fix to ward off fatigue and headaches and to increase concentration. Kicking the coffee habit can be hard for heavy users—in the worst cases it can cause withdrawal symptoms similar (though less severe) to those following quitting more serious addictions. The most common symptom (as any serious java junkie can attest) is a splitting headache, which starts pounding about a day after the last fix.

Coffee's effects also appear to be dependent on other drugs taken by the drinker. For instance, birth-control pills and some heart and ulcer drugs interfere with the body's ability to excrete caffeine, which heightens the impacts of even small doses. Nervous system stimulants, such as some appetite suppressants, asthma drugs, thyroid hormones, and oral decongestants, also magnify caffeine's effects. Not surprisingly, caffeine decreases the soothing effects of some tranquilizers such as Valium.

Caffeine is clearly a powerful drug, although coffee is far from the panacea it was considered in seventeenth-century England, when it was used to "cure" everything from dropsy, scurvy, and gout to nausea, flatulence, and vertigo. Its principal benefit is, simply, that it keeps us awake and active—which is important, as our ever-lengthening work hours are punctuated with increasing stress and decreasing leisure time. Its anti-headache properties—noted centuries ago—are still with us. Modern research has shown that caffeine dilates the blood vessels that feed the heart, increasing blood flow, while constricting blood vessels in the head, which helps to diminish even severe migraine headaches. Centuries-old pharmacological theories using coffee to treat asthma were also correct. Because they relax the smooth muscles (which help regulate our respiratory system), xanthines such as caffeine dilate the bronchioles in the lungs.

Scientific research on the physiological and psychological impacts of moderate coffee drinking has turned up very little evidence implying that the drink has seriously harmful effects. *Consumer Reports* maintains that "Caffeine is a little like a criminal suspect who's repeatedly pulled in for questioning, with the evidence always too thin to indict, but usually substantial enough to justify continued surveillance."[1]

Many studies published in the 1970s and early 1980s seemed to implicate coffee in everything from cancer of the bladder, pancreas, and breast; benign fibrocystic breast disease; and high cholesterol, to increased risk of heart attacks, premature births, and low birth weights. Further research revealed, however, that the lifestyle factors of heavy coffee drinkers frequently included unhealthy behavior such as cigarette smoking, which was often later found to be the chief culprit in these ailments.

More recent research has suggested that coffee may have a protective effect against liver cancer, type 2 diabetes, gallstone disease, kidney stones, cirrhosis, and, possibly, Alzheimer's and Parkinson's. Coffee has also been found to be a potent antioxidant, due in part to its intrinsic plant phenols and to compounds called melanoidins formed in the roasting process. In 2004, a series of studies (including one undertaken at the Nestlé Research Center in Lausanne) actually found that coffee was the single biggest contributor to total dietary intake of antioxidants.[2]

Coffee's impact on physical endurance has been exceedingly well documented since the days when the Galla used it in their prototypical energy bars. The institutionalization of the "coffee break" was designed to increase productivity by diminishing worker fatigue. Coffee can do this by "mobilizing" body fat and making it readily available to working muscles, which lengthens the time before the onset of fatigue. In fact, the International Olympic Committee considers caffeine a performance enhancer and screens athletes for excess amounts since it could confer an unfair advantage. However, because coffee also acts as a diuretic, stimulating urine production, drinking coffee before exercising can cause an athlete to become dehydrated more rapidly.

Coffee's role in raising cholesterol has been linked not to the caffeine itself but to the oil from the coffee beans. Using paper filters reduces the problem, however, presumably because the bean oils are trapped on the filter as the coffee passes through it. Because they do not utilize paper filters, French presses and espresso machines, along with a whole host of other brewing techniques, cannot boast such inadvertently healthful effects—on the other hand, they do produce better-tasting coffee.

Although studies have revealed conflicting findings, it appears that coffee does not incur any added cardiac risk for drinkers who consume fewer than about five cups of joe a day—even for those with cardiac arrhythmia or clogged arteries.

Female coffee drinkers will be relieved to hear that ongoing research has not confirmed a relationship between coffee and breast cancer, benign fibrocystic breast disease, or calcium loss. Happily, coffee consumption seems to reduce the risk of suicide, and, for drinkers who consume at least two cups per day, coffee's mood-enhancing properties include its ability to reduce irritability, improve mood, heighten social skills, and increase self-confidence and energy—properties that might explain why coffee is such a social drink and is often used in place of alcohol. Drinkers are also less likely to suffer from medical problems such as hypertension and diabetes, and are less likely to use anti-ulcer, anti-anxiety, anti-psychotic, or anti-hypertensive medications.

Whether or not coffee is found to have been healthful all along, the continuing interest in its effects is a testament to its centrality in our daily lives (and to the coffee industry's enthusiasm for rooting out good news). Coffee's pharmacological properties have always been at the heart of its appeal, but the secondary social structures that have evolved around its consumption have added additional layers of meaning to the coffee-drinking experience. While the office coffee break gives workers that important xanthenic boost, it is the social interaction—the gossip, the joking, and the idleness—that enables many workers to survive their tedious days and that forms the most appealing part of the ritual. Take a coffee break alone, and it's just a cup of coffee.

Throughout its history, the social aspects of coffee drinking have been at least as important as its direct physiological effects. The readiness of human societies to wrap this drug with a cloak of ritual and association has created fertile ground for marketeers. Coffee marketing rarely mentions the pharmacological aspects of the potion, instead concentrating on family life, social activities, and other heartwarming scenes that surround the preparation and consumption of coffee. A habit-forming drug that is widely accepted, even encouraged, and lends itself to conviviality and sophistication in equal measure would, indeed, seem to be the ideal product.

Branding the Brew

With the worldwide commercialization of everyday life that began in earnest in the nineteenth century appropriating everything from underwear to luncheon meat, it is not at all surprising that coffee drinking has grown from a homespun, immediately local affair into an international big business. During this great age of merchandising, coffee's promise was too good to pass up. Mass production, modern distribution, and "scientific" marketing techniques proved adept at homogenizing and popularizing the coffee experience by providing a consistent product and, of course, a handy drug-delivery system.

In a sense, it was this drug-delivery idea (either expressed or inherent in companies' approaches to their product) that eventually made a mockery of coffee's social role. Later "innovations," including instant coffee and caffeine-heavy soft drinks, cut into a good portion of coffee's constituency without, until recently, providing the traditionally rich, satisfying coffee experience that the remainder craved.

Although commercial roasting first appeared in New York at the end of the seventeenth century, it was considered a luxury and remained available only where population densities made it feasible. Until the late nineteenth century, consumers usually drank their coffee in coffeehouses or roasted their own.

Coffee was drunk widely, but its flavor was inconsistent, and it was often adulterated. As was the case for most other consumer products during this period, it was *caveat emptor*. Coffee was bought from local grocers or jobbers and was often excellent; just as often, it was foul and suspect. "Coffee" could contain any number of ingredients. Some were relatively benign, even charming, like the chicory that became popular in the South, where a taste developed for it during the Civil War when foreign coffee was hard to get; a regional preference for coffee with chicory survives to this day in New Orleans. But, unknown to drinkers, roast coffee could also include figs, dirt, dried blood, and worse.

In this melee, a few opportunistic, clever, and lucky entrepreneurs were able to create brands around quality and consistent product. In 1865 (a year after the invention of the first large commercial coffee roaster), John Arbuckle marketed the first commercially-available packages of ground, roasted coffee—Ariosa—thereby expanding his potential market well beyond the immediate environs of his roasting facility. Others followed suit and, developing into regional roasters, these companies were the ancestors of many of the mass-market coffees available today.

Early coffee companies were typical of newly developing American enterprise in their time. Centered around charismatic, driven founders, they were actively laying the foundation for mass consumer culture. Folgers Coffee, for example, was founded by a Nantucket Yankee in San Francisco (somewhat of a departure from the norm, as most of the other major coffee companies, indeed companies period, were founded in the East and spread west). The young Jim Folger, in a made-for-TV story showcasing grit and the vicissitudes of fortune, pioneered his business of selling roasted and ground coffee to gold miners, who took to the convenience of not having to roast and grind their own. During the California gold rush, ships transporting miners from

Central America (where they crossed the narrow isthmus after a sea journey from the eastern United States) to San Francisco made that city the first U.S. port to receive regular and large shipments of Central American coffee. The port also received coffee from the Dutch East Indies in bags marked with their origin: JAVA. This word was soon adopted to mean coffee in general. The West Coast has retained a preference for coffees from these origins ever since (which accounts, in part, for their popularity in the modern specialty coffee explosion—another nationwide coffee phenomenon with West Coast roots).

Companies such as Folgers, Arbuckle's, Hills Brothers, Maxwell House, and Eight O' Clock were all well established before World War I. They provided customers with a consistent product packaged for convenient use in the home. By the dawn of the twentieth century, these regional roasters were expanding rapidly. They developed innovative packaging (the vacuum pack—Hills Bros.), new marketing techniques (directly to grocers—Folgers), powerful advertising slogans ("Good to the Last Drop"—Maxwell House), tempting giveaways (Arbuckle's), and national distribution. This was the golden age of the independent coffee company and of many of the innovations that are now so ubiquitous.

Among these is decaffeinated coffee, which was brought to America in 1909 by Ludwig Roselius, who had been selling it under patent in Germany. One year later, Merck and Company sold the first decaf product in the United States: Dekafa. Immediately popular with those concerned by coffee's powerful punch, decaf was quickly adopted by all of the large coffee-roasting companies and soon found its way onto the shelves of all the major grocery store chains. After peaking at about 25 percent in the 1980s, today about 13 percent of the coffee drunk in the United States is decaf.

All of this activity had the dual effect of concentrating the roasting and distribution of coffee in a few regional companies (a hint of things to come on a global scale), and greatly increasing the per-capita consumption of coffee in the United States. Coffee's place at America's table was cemented during World War I, when it became an important part of the rations supplied to U.S. troops in Europe. This military market exposed an entire generation to coffee (and chewing gum and cigarettes), and there was no looking back, at least not until another generation switched to soda pop half a century later.

Coffee was undergoing a parallel institutionalization back home, where the United States was becoming a country of factory and office workers. Indoors, away from the rhythm of the seasons, the new America increasingly moved to the rhythm of machines. Here, coffee was the ideal drink: it gave that kick you needed to spend sixteen hours tightening screws on a mind-numbing, dangerous factory floor or pounding away at a keyboard. Coffee has always been the perfect complement to dehumanizing industrialization. "Their stimulant properties made . . . coffee . . . and tea the ideal drugs for the Industrial Revolution," argued drugologist Terence McKenna. "They provided an energy lift, enabling people to keep working at repetitious tasks that demanded concentration. Indeed, the tea and coffee break is the only drug ritual that has never been criticized by those who profit from the modern industrial state."[3]

The coffee break was quickly institutionalized, with employers providing the drug and unions demanding the regimented break. During the coffee break, everyone is happy: the company gets refreshed, stimulated workers, and the employees get a little moment of socialization and relaxation (not to mention a chance to feed their addiction). For the most part, the coffee break has been a rare point of agreement between workers and employers, although misanthropic managers occasionally attempt to eliminate coffee breaks in favor of the quick deskbound caffeine shot— barbarism routinely shown to be less effective at increasing worker output and satisfaction, yet one often self-imposed by harried and insecure office workers.

Abandoning the break and just having the coffee is the reduction of the ritual to bare drug-taking, and is grim to say the least.

Not surprisingly, coffee companies have always taken a keen interest in the coffee break, promoting it through advertising, research, and office coffee-service products. One 1998 coffee company-sponsored study, for example, estimated that half of Boston commuters take coffee breaks during the day and that, of these, 74 percent find that these breaks help relieve stress, even though half of those who do take coffee breaks didn't even leave their desks.[4]

By the 1920s coffee had become a universal beverage in America, enjoyed by rich and poor, young and old, men and women. It leapt across all social boundaries with remarkable ease and was equally at home on the factory floor and at the country club. Indeed, the coffee served at each of these establishments was (and occasionally remains) identical. This democratic appeal further delighted coffee marketers and roasters, who eventually created homogenized blends that would appeal to all and that, until the 1990s, obliterated class and other barriers within the coffee market.

Beginning around the time of World War I, and continuing on and off until today, consolidation, first within industries and then across them, became the rule of the day. Vast conglomerated enterprises emerged in many countries, the forerunners of today's transnationals. Companies grew and diversified—or swallowed up competitors—with an unprecedented fervor. This created a great and ongoing shakeout in the coffee sector, which had long been profitable but was populated by numerous small actors.

First, regional roasters developed national presences, edging out smaller competitors. Then, as waves of consolidation spread throughout the booming U.S. industrial economy, these companies themselves were absorbed by ever-larger conglomerates. In 1928, for example, emerging food conglomerate General Foods bought Maxwell House, just in time for the Great Depression that brought everything to a halt. In the postwar period, consolidation resumed when Procter & Gamble (P&G) bought Folgers in 1963, starting a coffee-brand feeding frenzy that continued through 1985, when Nestlé acquired Hills Brothers and MJB—two of the last, fiercely independent holdouts from the nineteenth century. Brand trading continued through 1999 when Sara Lee bought both of those companies as well as Chock full o' Nuts and Chase & Sanborn. Today, the fate of these four companies is undetermined, as Sara Lee announced in early 2005 a new transformation plan that includes divesting all of their U.S. supermarket coffees.

According to Oscar Schisgall, author of a sycophantic history of P&G, the coffee sector was simply too vibrant for the growing food conglomerates to ignore:

> What persuaded [P&G executive Howard Morgens] to lead P&G into the coffee business was an impressive array of facts presented at a 1963 meeting of P&G executives. "The total coffee business in this country, measured in retail dollar sales," Morgens said, "is approximately the same size as the total soap and detergent business [P&G's mainstay]." And there were other statistics to whet P&G's interest. The Pan American Coffee Bureau estimated that coffee was the country's largest food import. Over 70 percent of the U.S. population drank coffee, and an average of three cups were consumed per person per winter day.
>
> So large a market could not be ignored, he maintained, by a company already in the food business. Was coffee a syn-

Procter & Gamble Company

2004 Revenues: $56.7 billion
Employees: 110,000
Brands: Folgers, Millstone

P&G is the world's largest household products company and the world's largest advertiser. Founded by a pair of Cincinnati candlemakers in 1837, the company grew steadily, propelled by its innovative flagship products Ivory, Crisco, and Tide and by its aggressive marketing (Ivory was one of the earliest mass-market campaigns, and P&G's sponsorship of daytime radio dramas—"soap operas"—beginning in the 1930s was innovative and effective). After spending the postwar period seeking out and buying food companies that had distinguished themselves nationally—including Folgers coffee, which it acquired in 1963—P&G turned its attention to health-care products in the 1980s. Still, more than 4 percent of P&G's revenues comes from coffee, as it retains a 35 percent share of the U.S. coffee market.

In the 1990s, P&G focused on its core businesses of detergents, diapers, shampoo, and tampons. Through this focus, and a little downsizing and internal consolidation, P&G has increased sales by 40 percent and doubled its profits since 2000. In 2005, when P&G merged with Gillette, it had seventeen different billion-dollar brands, one of which is Folgers, and thirteen additional brands worth more than $500 million each.

ergistic product for Procter & Gamble? It was indeed. It was a low-price item quickly and steadily consumed. It was distributed by the grocery trade with which the company constantly dealt. P&G researchers had experience with blending flavors. And the buying department was highly proficient in the purchase of a wide range of commodities which, like green coffee, were subject to extreme price fluctuations.[5]

Playing Coke to Folgers' Pepsi, Maxwell House had, until the 1980s, consistently been the leading coffee brand in the United States. Developed in 1892 for the Maxwell House Hotel in Nashville, it quickly became a national brand and acquired its famous "Good to the Last Drop" slogan in 1907 (the phrase was allegedly coined by Theodore Roosevelt). The company was bought by General Foods in 1928. Subsequently, in 1985, GF was bought by Philip Morris, and ten years later it merged with Kraft, which Philip Morris had bought in 1988. (Philip Morris renamed itself the Altria Group in 2003.) In the early 1980s Folgers assumed leadership of the market as Maxwell House miscalculated just how badly it could mistreat its customers by abandoning even the semblance of quality. Now, the largest coffee brand in the country is owned by a soap company, while its major competitor is owned by a combined cereal and cheese company that is owned by a cigarette company. It isn't hard to see why this system has provided us with such bad coffee.

As parts of larger industrial empires, the major coffee companies became brands devoid of regional character or attachment. Since the 1980s, for example, both Folgers and Hills Brothers have closed their roasting facilities in San Francisco, their original home. Today, few consumers could identify the place of origin of most of the mass-market brands they consume, yet the most venerable often originated from very distinctive, regional companies.

As regional coffees were turned into national brands, the priorities of their producers changed. Localized taste preferences became less important and consistency in price, packaging, and flavor came to the fore. In order to buffer against changing world supplies of various types of coffee, roasters adopted diversified blends that they could adjust to keep price and taste relatively uniform even as supply conditions changed. While this strategy did indeed achieve consistency, it did so at the price of forsaking the diversity of flavors and qualities that had been the hallmark of the small independent roasters.

These conglomerates had the clout to be actors on the world stage. Through their lobbying group, the National Coffee Association (NCA), they attained their greatest political victory in 1962 with the establishment of the International Coffee Agreement (ICA). Through symbiotic relationships with producing country organizations such as Colombia's FNC, these multinationals—Nestlé in particular—expanded their operations into globally ubiquitous brands. In fact, even in many coffee-producing countries coffee is usually consumed as Nescafé.

The year 1962–63, the watershed in U.S. coffee history,

Nestlé SA

2004 Revenues: $70 billion
Employees: 247,000
Brands: Nescafé, Taster's Choice

Nestlé is the world's largest food conglomerate. Originating in Vevey, Switzerland, in 1843 as an infant-formula manufacturer, Nestlé's history is a series of mergers and acquisitions that inexorably drove it to ever-larger scales of operation. During World War I Nestlé entered the market in the Americas, which had not been diminished by hostilities, unlike its home market in Europe. Through its Brazilian operations, this led to the development of Nescafé in 1938—the first commercially-available soluble instant coffee.

Nestlé continued to grow in the postwar period and, by buying Carnation in 1985, launched the frenzy of hyper-consolidation that marked the 1980s for the food industry. Today, Nestlé employs nearly a quarter of a million people in over a hundred countries.

Though the company insisted until 1989 that voting shares could be held only by Swiss nationals, Nestlé has traditionally been quite global in its operations strategy.

Perhaps because it originated in a small country, Nestlé was among the first of the conglomerates to seek global sales aggressively. So much so that, by the 1960s, while other coffee roasters were fighting to keep Brazilian-made instant coffee out of the U.S. market, Nestlé was building Brazilian instant coffee plants. Nestlé still leads the way in building processing capacity in producing countries (which also happen to be some of its major consumers), including an instant coffee factory in Vietnam and coffee manufacturing and, since the late 1990s, marketing activities in China, which Nestlé had left in 1943.

Nescafé continues to be its flagship coffee and remains the world's largest coffee brand and the biggest beverage brand after Coca-Cola and Pepsi. The company estimates that, worldwide, 3,600 cups of Nescafé are drunk every second.

But even here coffee may not remain king for long: Nestlé's seventy brands of bottled water now account for nine percent of the company's sales, the same as soluble coffee. And the value chain for water is about as spare as it gets: pump, filter, bottle, sell.

marked both the largest per capita and the largest absolute coffee consumption. Americans drank an average of almost 40 gallons of coffee per person that year. It also marked the culmination of the coffee company buying spree by large conglomerates and the signing of the ICA—the international manifestation of the coffee-industrial complex that had developed in the United States. It was also the last time U.S. coffee consumption represented more than half of global consumption, with imports of 3.2 billion pounds of green coffee.

In the postwar period coffee companies were very profitable for their parent conglomerates. Packaging coffee in cans or bags and distributing it through nationwide networks to supermarkets, these brands competed fiercely with one another in their advertising campaigns but not in their pricing. Eventually, even the product itself became secondary. As brand competition took the near-exclusive form of advertising in a saturated market, the coffee industry became a parody of a functioning free market. This trend, combined with the industry's comfortable profit margins—and their inclination to keep them that way— had inevitable effects on the quality of coffee available to the consumer. Ever-cheaper beans were used, including cheap, harsh-tasting African robustas. Shorter roast times were employed in order to reduce the weight loss in roasting, which permitted the poor quality of the beans to shine through.

The homogenization and technification of coffee reached its nadir in the development of instant coffee in 1938. Instant coffee was a technification of the coffee marketing process that paralleled a broader trend toward mega-scale, industrialized, mass-market production in the postwar period. It was part of the same wave that included prefab houses, TV dinners, nylon stockings, and plastic of all kinds; it remains the Spam of hot drinks. In the postwar boom of quantity over quality, and the nationwide embrace of convenient consumption, instant coffee found a ready market. Sexy and modern, instant coffee eventually grew to represent 34 percent of coffee drunk in the United States in 1978, its peak year. Today it accounts for about 19 percent of supermarket coffee sales.

If in retrospect the coffee industry appeared to be out of its collective mind in pursuing the race for low quality, it is worth remembering that this blind love affair with consistency and technology was part of a larger cultural embrace of a mass-market modernism that set the second half of the twentieth century apart from all other periods in human history. Instant coffee was created by the same technophilia that later produced technified cultivation systems. During coffee's golden age in the United States—which coincided with the United States' golden age on Earth—this movement undoubtedly reached its purest, most hubris-laden form, as reflected in this 1962 gem from a coffee trade journal:

> Having come such a long, long way with the coffee industry and the worlds of engineering and chemistry, is it really unusual that the ultimate question should be asked . . . "how about a completely synthetic product?" After all, the average young adult of today does not even remember a time when there were no plastics, no synthetic fabrics . . . even, no instant coffee! . . . Research, over the past ten years, aimed at discovering and returning to the instant product those elusive components that make for the full flavor and aroma of the natural brew, has borne fruit . . . a fruit already anticipating its own harvest to come. . . .
>
> The questions [sic] that then, naturally arises is; if the natural brew can be reproduced so that the instant tastes and smells exactly like coffee, why add it to any

Market Share of U.S. Supermarket Coffee

Source: Information Resources, 2005

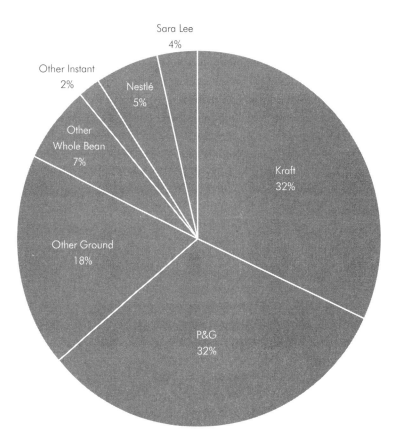

- Sara Lee 4%
- Other Instant 2%
- Nestlé 5%
- Other Whole Bean 7%
- Kraft 32%
- Other Ground 18%
- P&G 32%

coffee variety[?] The next, logical step, would be to add it to a much cheaper substance . . . such as any kind of roasted grain. . . . But, whether or not a goatherd named Kaldi, ever really danced with his aromatic charges; and regardless of whether the descendants of John Glenn drink synthetic coffee on their way to Andromeda . . . coffee, per se, certainly deserves a place in the drinking annals of mankind.[6]

Instant coffee continues to be popular in new coffee markets, particularly those that had traditionally been dominated by tea. This is most notably the case with Japan and the postwar United Kingdom, both of which have only relatively recently (since 1950) begun to experience growth in coffee consumption. In the United Kingdom in particular, in spite of a recent interest in specialty coffees (London now has more Starbucks branches than New York), 86 percent of the coffee consumed continues to be instant. The coffee industry now views instant as something of a stepping-stone from tea to coffee because of seeming similarities of preparation (apparently the coffee industry knows little about the elaborate Japanese and English tea ceremonies) and is now using instant coffee to establish a beachhead in China. There, Nestlé has introduced an instant coffee premixed with powdered milk and sugar in a bid to wean consumers from tea, a quickie that is becoming popular with the nation's growing urban middle class and schoolchildren in particular.

Still, there is a limit to what the consumer will swallow—especially without advertising. In the 1980s, Maxwell House took the dilution of its product one step too far, further reducing its quality and cutting back on advertising. In four years, Maxwell House lost its market dominance, and by 1989 its market share had fallen to 19 percent, well behind Folgers' 32 percent. In that year, after losing over $40 million, Maxwell House (formerly responsible for a third of General Foods' operating profit) quietly reformulated its blend in a bid to regain its former market dominance. In the 1990s it also renewed its marketing efforts, with a 27-percent

U.S. Coffee Drinking

Source: NCA, ICO—1992 and 1994 data extrapolated (survey not conducted)

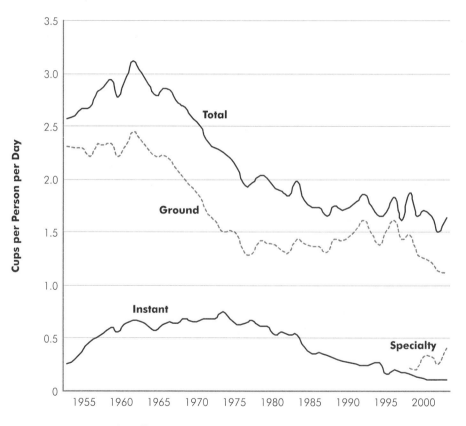

Note: Specialty coffee included in ground coffee prior to 1999.

spending increase (to $134 million) in 1996. By 2005, Maxwell House had recovered to claim roughly 30 percent of the flagship ground coffee market, trailing Folgers by just a hair.

With indistinguishably bland flavor profiles in the postwar period, the multinational mega-coffee companies competed soley by means of advertising and discounts, managing to strip coffee of most of its charm and appeal. The consistent loser in these battles, of course, was the coffee drinker.

This has particularly been the case in the United States, where supermarket swill dominated the market quickly and thoroughly. In Europe, many countries retained a higher coffee standard even as the multinationals moved in. In some cases, such as the Scandinavian countries, this is attributable to a long-standing emphasis on quality in coffee, such that even supermarket brands are held to the standards associated with expensive specialty coffee elsewhere—the mass-market leader there, Kraft's Gevalia, qualifies as a specialty coffee in North America. In other cases, such as Italy, the patterns of coffee consumption—more public, and more often espresso at coffee bars rather than in the home—precluded the rise to dominance of uniform and poor coffee.

In some European countries, like the UK and Russia, however, the story has been just the opposite. In countries that traditionally drink tea, "coffee" has usually meant a weak cup of sugary, milky Nescafé. The drive to supplant the native caffeine delivery system in these countries has only begun to make fine coffees available. Ironically, while coffee may be the predatory beverage in tea-drinking countries, in the United States progress in the caffeine experience has made coffee the victim of a similar displacement—one brought about largely by the industry's own neglect of its customer.

In the 1960s the introduction of mass marketed freeze-dried instant coffee—more expensive but more reminiscent of actual coffee—continued the trend of coffee-

**Altria Group
(formerly Philip Morris,
parent company of Kraft)**

2004 Revenues: $89.6 billion

Employees: 156,000

Brands: Maxwell House, Gevalia,
Sanka, General Foods
International Coffees, Maxim,
Yuban, Jacob (Europe's largest)

The world's largest cigarette purveyor saw
the writing on the wall and during the
1980s decided to diversify away from its
addictive and blatantly damaging flagship
product. But, considering tobacco's profitability, it did not diversify all that much: 64
percent of sales continued to be from
tobacco in 2004. Instead it just adopted a
name seemingly calculated to connote
absolutely nothing.

   Philip Morris (the person) opened a
tobacco shop in London in 1847. Through
a series of acquisitions, the company
moved to the United States in 1909, where
it focused on tobacco to become, through
its Marlboro brand, the world's leading cigarette producer. In 1970 Philip Morris

product technification. At the time, consumers of instant coffee readily acknowledged that instant coffee really did not taste like coffee but that its appeal was in the quick and easy preparation.

These fickle consumers, clearly, were ripe for the picking by anyone who could produce an even more convenient caffeine-delivery system. That system was the soft drink. While not new to the scene, soft drinks enjoyed a dramatic increase in market share beginning in the 1960s as consumption of the fizzy, sugary children's treat spread to new realms. Young adults—the infamous baby boomers—took to soda as an alternative to stodgy, boring coffee. Coffee was the limpid beverage of domination, warm and conformist and drunk on the job, be it in factory or office.

Mass-market coffee remained a steadfast promulgator of the old social paradigm, even while the society around it was changing radically. Around 1962, just when Old Coffee's power was at its height, the bean was part of the dominating cultural style that kept women in the kitchen and their husbands at work, at least according to the ads.

The tendency of the major roasters to demean women in their ads was strange, considering that women were their major customers. Still, well into the 1980s, P&G stuck with Folgers' Mrs. Olsen, the Scandinavian caterer who would mysteriously appear in the kitchen to help inept housewives salvage their marriages with a can of "mountain grown" coffee.

In her book *Soap Opera: The Inside Story of Procter & Gamble*, Alecia Swasy recounts:

"It was known as the 'there, there' campaign," said Miner Raymond, who helped develop the ads. P&G researched the campaign to see "how ugly and aggressive we could get in the ads," he admitted. Data showed that women "would accept as reasonable all sorts of abuse" in ads because many of them heard it at home.

In a recent [early nineties] Folgers "best part of wakin' up" ad, the husband gets out of bed to make the coffee. But he does it to make up for a fight he and his wife had the night before. One sip of coffee, and they kiss and make up. The message: It's a big sacrifice for a man to do his wife's work, but she's easily placated.[7]

The coffee companies continued to view each other as their competition, and so were unafraid to make these onerous associations. Meanwhile, soda ads were young, hip, and happening, giving a thoroughly positive alternative to the bitter family dynamics of the television coffee household.

In the face of this attitude—almost intentionally alienating to that vast chunk of household coffee buyers who happen to be women—and a continually lackluster product, coffee consumption continued to decline. It was not until the late 1970s that the industry even realized where its real competition lay. At the end of that decade and throughout the 1980s, declining coffee consumption became so alarming that the National Coffee Association, the industry group that had once virtually dictated U.S.–Latin America economic policy, took to running goofy tel-

acquired Miller Brewing, and within a decade was, in addition to the world's largest cigarette company, its second-largest beer company. In 1985 Philip Morris bought General Foods for $5.6 billion (the second-largest buyout in history at that time) and, among other milestones, became the leading coffee roaster in the United States through its newly acquired Maxwell House brand. In 1988 it bought Kraft Foods and merged it with General Foods in 1995 to create Kraft General Foods. In 2000, it bought Nabisco, which was folded into Kraft. This food behemoth was floated in an IPO in 2001, with the parent company retaining 85 percent ownership. The next year, Philip Morris renamed itself the Altria Group, a perfectly generic and meaningless name for the entity that owns dozens of the most iconic brand names in American culture. In 2004 Kraft was responsible for roughly 30 percent of the ground roasted coffee market in the United States and was the market leader in seven European countries plus South Korea.

men! Don't let it come to this! Win your fight for a decent cup of coffee without losing your temper!

every man's right · every wife's duty

1962 Chock full o' Nuts ad. The small print below the bedraggled homemaker reads "A man's home is his castle! You have a right to good coffee in your home, and your wife has a duty to serve it. Don't be the victim of womanly penny-pinching! If your wife refuses to spend the few extra pennies for Chock full o' Nuts Coffee, she is denying you that deep-down contentment that only the heavenly coffee can bring you! Men, assert yourselves! Be calm, but firm! Tonight, take home a can of Chock full o' Nuts Coffee and tell your wife in a voice of command that this is the coffee you want in your home from now on!"

evision ads extolling the virtues of coffee like a latter-day Pasqua Rosée. "Coffee—Make a Break for It" spots depicted active, energetic music and sports stars doing their duties under the influence of the bean, and invited the viewer to join this generation of "Coffee Achievers."

The battle between the two stimulants broke out into the open in 1989, when Pepsi began to market a version of its dark concoction as a breakfast beverage. It ran TV ads depicting coffee drinkers as dull and confused, sleepy older men who drink the brew only because of "tradition," and calling Pepsi AM, its assault on the roasters' heartland, "The taste that beats coffee cold." Pepsi AM was even stocked in the coffee aisle in test markets.

The NCA, at the urging of Procter & Gamble, countered with an ad accusing Pepsi of being unhealthfully sugary, pointing out that drinking a can a day would be the equivalent of eating over 25 pounds of sugar in a year. "Coffee," the spot concluded, "the natural a.m. choice."

In her history of P&G, Alecia Swasy recounts the standoff:

P&G's Mark Upson, vice president of food and beverage, sent the tape and a letter to Pepsi. Upson said P&G would blanket the airwaves with the ad if Pepsi chose to continue attacking coffee. He also tried to use the muscle of the entire coffee industry trade group [the NCA] to get Pepsi to back off. It was a clear example of P&G using its clout and advertising muscle to intimidate competitors into retreating. . . . In the end, the whole effort by P&G seemed unnecessary, considering the lukewarm response Pepsi AM received from consumers, who considered its taste rather flat. By October 1990 Pepsi had scrapped the project.[8]

But it was too late. If cola has not yet succeeded in its assault on the breakfast table (Coke tried it and failed, too), it has clearly triumphed in many of the other traditional strongholds of coffee. The competing television ads hint at the underlying cause. Both products are corporate and mass-produced, to be sure, but coffee managed to appear tired and dull even in its own advertisements. The Pepsi spots were exciting and new; hip and knowing MTV material. The coffee ads seemed to be from another, duller era, with a hokey game show script and bland production values.

While P&G was appealing to the growing health consciousness of U.S. consumers in its focus on sugar, the soda companies had already jumped into this breach with a panoply of diet colas. Today, the workplace is littered with Diet Coke, the most convenient caffeine delivery system short of No-Doz.[9]

In the United States coffee has long been viewed as an adult drink. Like tobacco and alcohol, coffee is perceived as a pleasure unsuitable for children, to whose health it is considered detrimental by some. The switch in focus to soft drinks has allowed food-product conglomerates to sell stimulating caffeine beverages to ever-younger consumers, thus weaning them onto a caffeine habit earlier and locking them in to soda, again to the dismay of coffee producers.

While the roasters folded on this issue by declining to overtly push coffee on children, there was a time when they considered it—back when the soft-drink industry was the 99-pound weakling of the beverage market. "But what about the children who are not permitted to drink coffee because of the caffeine content?" asked W. A. Heyman, who had helped introduce instant coffee to the U.S. Army in 1941, but was evidently less of a visionary in 1963. "We have developed a pure coffee drink without caffeine—a pure carbonated coffee drink which is absolutely caffeine-free. This is a rare opportunity to afford children the delicious flavor of coffee. Here is a new potential market for the future generation. There is no better way to spend the 'advertising budget' than in the field of soft drinks. Soft drinks made of coffee."[10]

Actually, the idea had been around since the 1920s, but it took a muscular soft-drink company to attempt it on a large scale. In 1996 Pepsi took up Dr. Heyman's challenge, producing an experimental coffee soft drink: Pepsi Kona. It tested poorly and the project was shelved, although the idea keeps resurfacing: in 2005 Coke was reportedly planning to release a coffee soda named Blak, perhaps encouraged by Pepsi's successful partnership with Starbucks to market DoubleShot and Frappuccino ready-to-drink (i.e., canned or bottled) coffee drinks.

The paradoxical outcome has been, rather than decaffeinated coffee sodas, over-caffeinated coffee-free pop. In recent years, "power" drinks like Jolt and their newer, vitamin-infused cousins, caffeinated "energy" drinks like Red Bull, have become market sensations, creating a whole new industry that competes directly with coffee. These drinks appeal to an increasingly health-conscious younger demographic. Together with sports drinks (which, like Gatorade, focus on rehydration rather than performance enhancement), they represent 6 percent of the nonalcoholic beverage market. But with annual growth reaching almost 20 percent by 2004, they're the primary growth drivers in the category. Both Coke and Pepsi quickly entered this surging market, following the trail blazed by Red Bull.

Even in the early years of the new millennium, mainstream industry "innovation" wasn't up to this kind of competition. In the face of the worldwide glut of the Coffee Crisis, new initiatives consisted largely of new ways to obscure the over-extraction of inferior, under-roasted beans with steaming and flavor "enhancers." While the appeal of coffee may never make much sense to those who view it as little more than a daily stimulant, the regrettable truth is that for too long this had been the cynical attitude

U.S. Beverage Consumption

Source: USDA

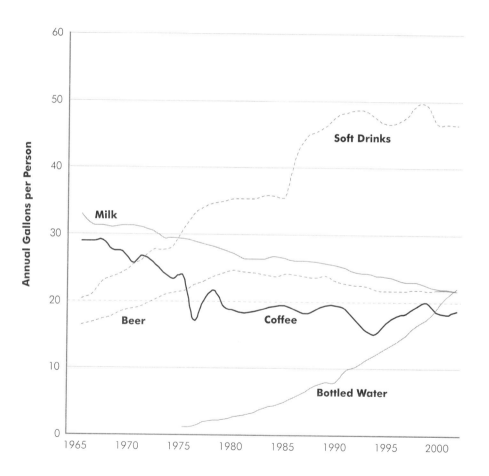

of the industry itself. The rest of us—those for whom even that gelding decaf is an elixir more agreeable than any soda or instant abomination—have been sold short. Fortunately, something is being done about it. While supermarket coffee, soda, and energy drinks continue their battle for "stomach share," more discerning coffee lovers have revolutionized the way society views the glorious cup.

5

The Specialty Coffee Boom

We would take something old and tired and common—coffee—and weave a
sense of romance and community around it. We would rediscover the mystique
and charm that had swirled around coffee throughout the centuries.

—Howard Schultz, Starbucks CEO (1997)

Upstarts

FORTUNATELY FOR AMERICAN COFFEE DRINKERS, the art of fine coffeemaking was kept alive throughout the dark ages in a few lonely outposts. A few very small roasters, mostly European immigrants, managed to obtain high-quality beans and make genuinely good coffee available in select markets throughout the bleak decades of 1950 to 1990. Found mostly in ethnic enclaves such as New York's Little Italy or counter-culture hubs like Greenwich Village and Berkeley, roasters such as the legendary Alfred Peet made available dark-roasted arabicas to small but ultimately influential sections of the public.

In 1962, mainstream coffee was at its peak. In the product life-cycle of Introduction, Growth, Maturity, and Post-Maturity (also known as Stagnation or Decline), coffee fully matured that year. Then consumption of the beverage ceased growing. From 1962 to the early 1990s, the subsequent phase of Stagnation was manifested in a gradual decline in per-capita coffee drinking, a tendency by the consumer to "stretch" coffee (in the late 1930s Americans extracted about forty-five cups from one pound of coffee; in the early 1990s this had grown to nearly one hundred cups, and price was the major determinant of consumer preference.

In the 1970s and 1980s coffee was increasingly battered by price spikes and by a growing popular fear that coffee-drinking is detrimental to human health. The price spike of 1975–77 in particular helped reduce subsequent demand, even after prices had fallen. In the 1980s coffee was implicated in certain cancers, although smoking, a behavior strongly associated with coffee drinking, was later found to be the guilty party. Nevertheless, this period saw the industry move onto the defensive, with the National Coffee Association (NCA) sponsoring extensive research into the health effects of coffee and running pro-coffee television spots.

Despite the best efforts of the industry, coffee continued to be viewed as an unexciting drink for fogies or, at best, one of those ubiquitous staples that make no cultural statement at all. The focus continued to be on price, particularly after the severe price shocks of the 1970s. In addition to its advertising efforts, the industry tried to increase coffee consumption by distributing "official" scoops and convincing consumers to brew stronger coffee. But all this came in the absence of any sort of flavor incentive; little effort was made to improve the quality of retail coffee.

In this not-very-promising milieu, a couple of Seattle coffee lovers under the sway of the fine brews of Peet's in Berkeley opened a small whole-bean coffee store called Starbucks in 1971. The Peet's/Starbucks connection has acquired a rare mystique among coffee enthusiasts. Alfred Peet was the mentor of Starbucks founders Jerry Baldwin and Gordon Bowker. In 1984, when both chains were about the same size, Starbucks bought Peet's. In 1987 the original owners of Starbucks sold their interests to Howard Schultz but kept Peet's. During Starbucks' aggressive expansion, the two agreed to keep out of each others' home markets for four years; until 1992 there were no Starbucks in Northern California. Now, Peet's is renowned for its coffee but Starbucks is ubiquitous.

The story of Starbucks is the story of a new way of looking at coffee, one as initially distinct from the world of multinational commodity deal-making as Starbucks' offerings were initially distinct from the generic canned blends that the conventional trade produced. But the new industry, now called "specialty coffee" and represented by its own trade groups contending with its own unique issues, developed in an eerily similar fashion to the mega-national industry it sought to usurp.

Specialty coffee, distinguished by an attention to quality and freshness, spent the 1970s and early 1980s slowly building a loyal customer base and spreading awareness of fine arabicas and darker roasts. Though obscured by a sea of weak robusta blends, fine coffee was there if you knew where to look; it could be had by mail order or in a few cosmopolitan centers.

In the 1980s the specialty coffee industry became more organized and, like retail roast coffee in the 1860s, entered a period of strong growth. In the case of Starbucks, the narrative parallels the story of Folgers with uncanny accuracy. Like Jim Folger, Howard Schultz rose out of East Coast poverty to create a new, successful life in the West. Like Folger, his genius lay in knowing what he was selling, and to whom.

Folger sold modern convenience to gold miners, and later housewives, in an era when not having to roast and grind your own coffee was a genuine relief in a life of toil. Schultz sold a comfortable, safe gathering place and a status symbol—a club, really—in a period of uncertainty and depersonalization. Much as Folger distinguished his product in an age of adulteration and fly-by-night operators by providing quality and consistency, Schultz provided a reliable, consistent brand in the midst of a proliferation of independent coffee shops. Schultz and his team were able to package the urbane café experience for a bourgeois clientele looking for the community and flavor of the Berkeley coffee shop without the underground scene or revolutionary politics. They did so under the now-familiar Starbucks logo, imposing rigid consistency and a brand name on the simple experience of visiting a coffee shop—an experience that had been known for individual variability, even quirkiness, in the past.

Again, like Folger, Schultz was a shrewd businessman and, perhaps more important, was in the right place at the right time. Both were able to build strong regional, then national, then international brands, and both became very, very rich.

But even as specialty's Growth period got under way, the large corporations paid scant attention to the new roasters and stores, say the marketing consultants Adrian Slywotzky and Kevin Mundt:

> Industry executives did not know how to respond. They spent millions on advertising to maintain share in the shrinking market. Perpetual rounds of discounting and millions of coupons did nothing to raise brand prestige. Despite constant price promotions, coffee was a supermarket loss leader every week. To make matters worse, the majors converted from 16- to 13-ounce cans, claiming the contents produced the same amount of coffee—a move consumers did not view as adding value.

The Big Three did not feel threatened by Starbucks cafés and a growing host of regional whole-bean roasters who were marketing their premium brands in supermarkets and specialty stores. Although these start-ups were experiencing double-digit growth rates, to the majors their total sales seemed minuscule. Starbucks' 1988 sales were $10 million. It was hard for the majors to measure or even imagine the

Espresso

Coffee extracted by pressurized water has been around since the nineteenth century, but the modern espresso machine was invented by Fernando Illy in 1904. To make espresso, water is heated to just below boiling, then forced by a piston through a crucible of packed, finely ground coffee. This short burst of water—when released properly by an inspired operator—extracts the volatile and flavorful oils from the coffee without undue bitterness. And it does it very quickly. Espresso was originally invented as a way for rushed Italian commuters to enjoy a fresh, hot coffee on the run.

Briefly popular during the 1960s, the resurgence of espresso in the United States in the 1990s has been accompanied by a general improvement in the quality of American coffee and a general darkening of roasts. Coffee for espresso is dark roasted and is blended to extract properly under the special conditions of the espresso machine. While most of the espresso drunk in the United States is obscured by milk in lattes and cappuccinos (so named because they resemble the garb of Capuchin monks), the acme of our favorite mind-altering substance is still the viscous, crema-capped *ristretto*.

momentum of such tiny numbers relative to a $5 billion industry. Also, having made several failed attempts at marketing gourmet coffee, the brand leaders falsely assumed that gourmet coffee was just a fad.[1]

But in the next few years, the specialty coffee trend caught on across the United States. Overnight, "coffee shops" became "cafés" and convenience stores and gas stations across the continent began to serve espresso (or, all too often, "expresso").

In 1994, when coffee prices broke out of the slump engendered by the effective end of the ICA, many in the specialty industry were taken by surprise. Weaned during a period of low prices and less able to hedge than the majors, for whom many different shipments of coffee are interchangeable, even Starbucks found itself exposed to serious financial risk. The rise of the specialty coffee industry had been partially incubated by low prices, but, when the weather turned bad, this new sector proved that it was here to stay. Rather than lose market share under higher prices—the usual course of events for industrialized coffee—its share continued to grow, as though unrelated to price. By 2004 retail specialty coffee in the United States—sold at some 18,000 cafés, roaster-retailers, kiosks, and carts—had reached $9.6 billion in sales. While specialty coffee is only about 17 percent of total domestic coffee consumption by volume, the sector has grown to command about half the value of the $19.2 billion U.S. coffee industry.[2]

Growth of Specialty Coffee

Source: SCAA, Starbucks

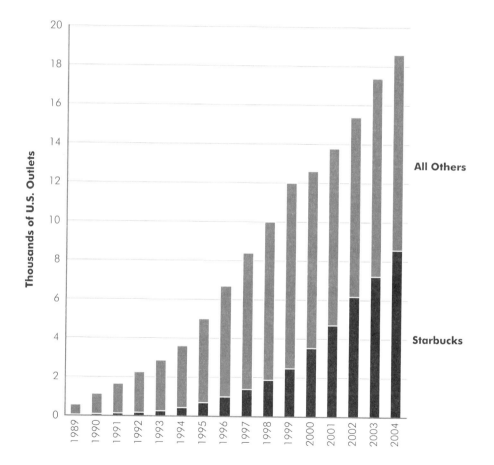

Thousands of U.S. Outlets

All Others

Starbucks

A New Landscape

An important aspect of this new industry is its relative decommodification of coffee. Where the conglomerates had been concerned only with price and consistency, this new industry considers origin, quality, processing, and cultivation methods as relevant qualities of the bean. It also extends the option of choosing roasts, grinds, and so on to the consumer, thus creating a much richer, personal coffee landscape and necessitating a structurally distinct trading system.

As specialty coffee's Growth phase got into full swing, it consolidated into a few dominant corporate brands: major presences like Starbucks, Peet's, Green Mountain, Diedrich, and others. The late 1990s saw a frenzy of acquisitions and mergers, which led to a specialty sector with a few large actors, many small companies, and hardly any medium-sized players. In this way, the coffee-bar sector has come to resemble the restaurant business, in which McDonald's competes with Joe's Diner on every street. If anything, specialty coffee is even more concentrated: today, almost half of all cafés in America are owned by Starbucks, but the vast majority of the remainder are small operators with fewer than three shops.

In spite of consolidation, this boom has seen an overall explosion in the number of U.S. roasters—the first reverse in a century. While the new micro-roasters are numerous, they nonetheless account for a very small proportion of U.S. roasting capacity. Still, while 60 percent of the coffee drunk in the United States in 2004 came from the four major roasters, this is down from a whopping 90 percent twenty years ago, in part because they've had to make room on the supermarket shelf for an increasing number of specialty brands, including Starbucks and Peet's.

In response, new, darker roasts have become available among the cans, as well as new, variously successful (or ridiculous) products such as Nestlé/Coca-Cola's Nescafé Ice Java Iced Coffee Syrup and the inelegantly named—and short-lived—Maxwell House Coffeehouse Iced Coffees. The majors have also introduced their own specialty coffee brands, such as Kraft's Gevalia and Chock full o' Nuts' cafés (actually a return to that company's 1940s business) and their short-lived Quikava drive-throughs. Nestlé even briefly sold whole-bean coffee under the Nescafé name at the start of the new millennium.

Good espresso is the perfect meeting of great coffee, shiny technology, and an obsessive barista.

But the majors had created coffee's poor image in the first place, and their direct forays into this new territory have been generally ill-conceived and hollow. The most effective entry strategy for them has been the old tactic of acquisition. In 1995 P&G acquired Millstone, a regional specialty roaster from the Pacific Northwest, and used its distribution muscle to quickly turn the brand into the second-largest specialty supermarket presence, with 2004 sales of $70 million. Eight O'Clock, the number one specialty supermarket brand with sales of $73 million, had arrived at its position from the opposite direction: since 1919 it had been the house brand of A&P supermarkets but was spun off in 2003 as a specialty brand. For their part, in 1998, Kraft signed an agreement with Starbucks to distribute the latter's marquee brand to supermarkets—an arrangement that yielded sales of $11 million in 2004. But swallowing Starbucks whole is probably not the majors' next step—after all, it is now a $6 billion company, and its core business is outside the majors' supermarket stomping grounds.

For the old-guard coffee sector, the growth of specialty coffee has been perplexing. After scratching their heads wondering why consumption had been declining since 1962 (and blaming the soft-drink companies), the mainstream roasters have

157

been struggling to get a footing in the new coffee sector. Although companies like General Foods laid some of the groundwork with the introduction of its International Coffees (flavored instant coffees) in 1973, and Colombia's FNC led the way in developing the idea that coffee from some origins is better than others, the revolutionary element of the new industry has been so far insurmountable. The very idea of a Maxwell House or Nescafé gourmet coffee is contradictory; their French roast or espresso roast is undermined by the very fact that it is vacuum-packed in cans or, worse, is instant.

Nonetheless, there is a substantial market for ersatz specialty coffee among supermarket coffee drinkers. In 2004, 10 percent of all coffee sold in supermarkets and mass retailers (excluding Wal-Mart) was whole bean.[3] Much of it fell in a middle ground: better than canned coffee but not up to gourmet standards. But at their worst, these coffees—whole beans in valve-sealed bags—superficially resemble gourmet coffee and yet are foul in the cup. And worst of all, some of these sell for prices comparable to truly great, fresh-roasted coffees available from real specialty shops.

Supermarkets and cafés aren't the only place to find allegedly gourmet coffee these days; it's also cropping up in unexpected places like gas station convenience stores (7-Eleven and Exxon Mobil stations, for example), as office coffee, and in donut mega-chains like Dunkin' Donuts. In 2005, even McDonald's announced plans to overhaul its tasteless effluent.

Meanwhile, the new specialty coffee players have tapped into the power of the coffee industry of old: in its diversity and focus on quality and distinctiveness, the specialty coffee industry is singularly profitable. Specialty beans that retail for $12 a pound are wholesaled (green) for about $2 a pound. As for cafés, profits seem to hover consistently around 20 percent—higher where there is more foot traffic, since the costs of pulling an additional shot of espresso are quite small once the retail location is established and there is a person behind the counter.

The Starbucks Phenomenon

The success of Starbucks, and by extension the entire specialty coffee industry in the United States, derives from two interrelated factors. Not only was the taste of its coffee a revelation to drinkers more used to fetid swill, but the coffee-drinking space itself neatly filled a yawning void in modern life. Cafés are a very old idea, but in the consumerist landscape of the 1980s they were a radical departure from the norm. They encouraged the customer to hang out, to idle away the afternoon, and to do so without paying very much. In a landscape of public spaces designed to entice people to buy things and then leave (including such frankly manipulative devices as fast food restaurants with colors designed to make you hungry and chairs designed to make you uncomfortable), a subdued public space with couches and books amounted to a radical revision of the consumer-retailer relationship. When Starbucks began to sell coffee drinks rather than just roasted beans, Schultz and his team noticed this need immediately:

> Americans are so hungry for a community that some of our customers began gathering in our stores, making appointments with friends, holding meetings, striking up conversations with other regulars. Once we understood the powerful need for a Third Place, we were able to respond by building larger stores, with more seating. In some stores, we hire a jazz band to play on weekend nights.
>
> While my original idea was to provide a quick, stand-up, to-go service in downtown office locations, Starbucks' fastest growing stores today are in urban or suburban residential neighborhoods. People don't just drop by to pick up a half-pound of

decaf on their way to the supermarket, as we first anticipated. They come for the atmosphere and the camaraderie.

The generation of people in their twenties [now in their thirties] figured this out before the sociologists. As teenagers, they had no safe place to hang out except shopping malls. Now that they are older, some find that bars are too noisy and raucous and threatening for companionship. So they hang out in cafés and coffee bars. The music is quiet enough to allow conversation. The places are well-lit. No one is carded, and no one is drunk.[4]

Schultz makes much of the "Third Place," a term coined by the sociologist Ray Oldenburg to describe the non-home, non-work environment that had once been the forum for public life but that had almost disappeared under the postwar regime of highly regimented schedules, commuter life, and television. This had clearly been the role of the old coffeehouses in Europe and had been present in America in the form of neighborhood gathering places such as bars and coffee shops. Disintegration of these spaces under the postwar regime was responsible, argues Oldenburg, for the anomie rampant in modern industrial civilization.

The need for a Third Place may account for the cultlike devotion of many Starbucks frequenters; the company reports that the average Starbucks customer visits eighteen times a month. In this loyalty, Schultz sees evidence of the realization of Oldenburg's vision. "If there is one message I wish to leave with those who despair of suburbia's lifeless streets," writes Oldenburg, "of the plastic places along our 'strips,' or of the congested and inhospitable mess that is 'downtown,' it is: It doesn't have to be like this!"[5]

Developing during a time of uncertain affluence in the early 1990s, specialty coffee was part of a larger trend that includes such developments as microbrewed beer, "rustic" breads, single-malt scotches, and organic vegetables. In each case, a consumer product has been recast as something more authentic, more traditional, diverse, flavorful, and healthful than the mass-produced product it supplants. In each case, the new "specialty" product is hyped as the original, traditional item that had been debased by mass production and corporatism. These goods come prepackaged with lifestyle signifiers that ironically reject the very systems that bring them to us.

The trends analyst Faith Popcorn describes the appeal of these products as deriving from their role as "Small Indulgences." A three-dollar latte is not, when viewed this way, an absurdly overpriced glass of hot milk. Rather, it is a quick and cheap vacation, a break from the hectic modern lifestyle. What's more, it's one that almost everyone can afford and is small enough to not be overtly indulgent or decadent. "In a consumer culture," writes Popcorn, "the motive has never been need, but want. Pushing that motivation beyond want to deserve is a recent, and powerful, cultural transformer."[6]

By providing a viable Third Place lubricated with a Small Indulgence, the specialty coffee industry has established a powerful link. Drinking a rare, dark roasted coffee at home or work evokes, by association, the community of the café. Similarly, merely being in a café becomes a Small Indulgence. The fact that both features of specialty coffee were initially defined by their distinction from the dominant corporate culture of the American Century reinforces their association further, and makes any overt old-line intrusions into the industry—Maxwell House Coffeehouse Roast, Folgers French Roast—ring false by definition.

Starbucks and the rest of the specialty coffee industry have developed a love-hate relationship for this reason. As Starbucks has grown, it has turned into a large corporation. Its senior staff members now include people who learned the tricks of the trade at Nike, Burger King, McDonald's, and 7-Eleven. It is making consolidated net revenues averaging around $17 million a day at some 10,000 stores worldwide. It has partnered with the big boys: PepsiCo, Anheuser-Busch, United Airlines, Marriott,

Hewlett-Packard, and Barnes & Noble. It has, in many ways, become the antithesis of the independent specialty coffeehouse, providing a corporatized, homogenized retail experience with a consistent but not outstanding product. In fact, coffee itself is becoming less and less important to what has become more of a lifestyle brand than simply a coffee company.

This has proved to be a critical element in the company's continued growth. Supply and logistical considerations make it impossible to extend the artisanal gourmet coffee ethic to 10,000 shops around the world. As the company has grown, the quality of its coffee has inevitably declined. The Starbucks experience was once characterized by hard-line coffee snobbery: in the beginning the whole-bean shop refused to even sell coffee drinks, and even after Howard Schultz took over and its expansion began, the company eschewed flavorings of any sort. But, as it has entered the mass marketplace, this stance has quietly given way to a more pragmatic ethos that embraces the Pumpkin-Spice Latte, the Mint Mocha Chip Frappuccino, and even something known as a Strawberries and Crème Frappuccino Blended Crème. Worldwide distribution from four roasting plants—three in the United States (Washington, Pennsylvania, Nevada), and one in Amsterdam—means that, in spite of advances in vacuum-pack technology, true freshness can no longer be central to Starbucks' identity. And with more than 300 hundred million pounds roasted each year, the brand is by definition too big to feature truly rare coffees.

Instead, Starbucks trades on its ubiquity and on the carefully stewarded basket of social signifiers it embodies. Unlike coffee, these corporate attributes can be extended to other consumer products. In recent years, for example, Starbucks has entered the entertainment world. Its Hear Music acquisition lets customers buy compilation CDs, listen to Starbucks-selected music on satellite radio, and even burn their own discs at in-store kiosks. The good taste that customers attribute to Starbucks in the world of coffee lets them trust the corporation's musical taste as well, as though it were their hip friend—the one who first turned them on to the secret of French roast. And with the sort of demographic sensitivity that makes Starbucks so attuned to its social environment, the results have been highly profitable: collaborations with various record labels have resulted in skyrocketing album sales. When Ray Charles's posthumous *Genius Loves Company* went triple-platinum in 2004, a quarter of the sales were at Starbucks stores. In 2005, the company took it a step further and became the exclusive distributor of a CD of Bob Dylan tunes recorded in 1962 at the Gaslight Café in Greenwich Village—an album that had previously been available only as a bootleg. It was symbolic closure, highlighting just how far both popular music and the café scene had come from the days when Dylan had been a mainstay at underground coffeehouses in the 1960s.

Yet these are exactly the kinds of coffeehouses that Starbucks' growth has long threatened. If the prepackaged lifestyle toolkit of a Starbucks CD is a godsend to suburban consumers who don't have ready access to authentic social networks of their own, in many areas Starbucks is competing directly with the kind of small, independent cafés that define the specialty coffee movement. To these Third Places, the gathering spots of genuine local community, Starbucks itself is that "plastic place along our strips."

Starbucks' tactics in moving into established café territory have been roundly condemned not only because of the inevitable damage to an area's unique character but because of the hostile tactics the company sometimes uses to barge into such communities. The coffee giant is frequently accused of approaching the landlords of independent cafés and making them offers they can't refuse, going so far as to buy buildings that they have targeted for Starbucks locations. This has stimulated a Starbucks backlash that has prevented or postponed new stores from opening in a number of places. But overall, the Starbucks juggernaut continues with little pause.

Perhaps the greatest and most threatened café neighborhood is Europe itself. In

Starbucks Corporation

2004 Net Revenues: $5.3 billion
Employees: 96,000

Founded in Seattle in 1971, Starbucks began life as a bean sales–only shop catering to serious coffee afficionados. In 1987 it was acquired by Howard Schultz, formerly an executive at the small (eight-shop) company. Seized by an espresso-fueled epiphany while in Milan, Schultz developed its now-familiar formula, and expanded it aggressively.

Today Starbucks is the undisputed café chain king, owning and operating some 10,000 outlets around the world. It has entered into joint marketing programs with other leading corporate giants, including PepsiCo (bottled Frappuccino), Dreyer's (coffee ice cream), Barnes & Noble (in-store cafés), Host Marriott (airport concessions), Capitol Records (compilation CDs of café music), HP and T-Mobile (in-store Wi-Fi), and United Airlines (in-flight coffee), and now competes directly with the old guard by retailing whole and ground coffee beans in supermarkets. Expanding beyond

1998 Starbucks acquired the London-based (and American-founded and -owned) Seattle Coffee Company for $83 million and announced its plan to turn the company into Starbucks' European beachhead. By 2005, from a base of 474 Starbucks outlets in the UK, the company was actively moving into traditional coffee strongholds like France and Germany—a quarter of the company's European stores were on the continent in that year. Though total European stores, including the UK, comprised not much more than a tenth of Starbucks' stores outside North America, this region is sure to be among the company's biggest growth areas as it marches toward its stated goal of 25,000 outlets worldwide—approaching the ubiquity of McDonalds, which had more than 30,000 restaurants in 2004.

This is the latest chapter in the American genius for marketing: in the United States Starbucks is seen as the heir to an ancient European tradition of coffee, but in Europe it is a chic American cultural import. Indeed, while espresso may be an Italian innovation, "to go" coffee is unquestionably American: it was first introduced by 7-Eleven in the 1940s and, at a million cups a day, remains that company's best-selling beverage.

If Starbucks is repackaging an ancient tradition in Europe, it is contributing to cultural imperialism in Asia, where it has been expanding its presence relatively aggressively, competing head-to-head with market-expansion efforts by the likes of Nestlé. Starbucks' 1,100 stores there are winning over affluent urban dwellers in traditionally tea-drinking communities, skipping the instant coffee approach to coffee imperialism long championed by the old guard. In these environments, ironically, espresso and lattes aren't Italian at all—they're as American as Coca-Cola. In Indonesia's five Starbucks outlets, bags containing Indonesian beans that have been shipped to North America for roasting and back again are labeled "product of the U.S.A."

While Starbucks has been unafraid to ride roughshod over vibrant local coffee scenes, it has produced the undeniable benefit of greatly expanding consumer awareness of specialty coffees. It is thanks to Starbucks that espresso, lattes, and the like are familiar drinks outside Italy. Many of its cafés are the only coffeehouses in the suburban malls that comprise the Third Places in America's fastest-growing regions—places where espresso might still be unknown were it not for the chain. If in the process too many Americans have come to associate Starbucks' milky concoctions with quality coffee, at least the Frappuccino is more likely to be the gateway to true connoisseurship than what passed for coffee in the past.

Starbucks is even reaching a point where it is broadening the demographic exposed to specialty coffee. As the company grows it is finding pent-up demand, as the success of dozens of Starbucks stores at Magic Johnson's inner-city entertainment complexes demonstrate.

Love it or hate it, the Starbucks phenomenon is certainly awe-inspiring. Serendipitously located at the nexus of a number of different cultural trends, this company—and the rest of the specialty coffee industry—has led a charmed life and changed forever the ways in which we engage with this compelling and

coffee to become more of a lifestyle brand, it has launched an entertainment division, acquiring Hear Music, and has recently entered the bottled-water business with its purchase of Ethos Water.

ancient drink. It is quite likely that the world of coffee a few decades hence will be unrecognizable to those who suffered though the bitter, watery decades that preceded the coffee-bar explosion. It may already be.

"I'll Have a Double Tall Low-Fat Soy Orange Decaf Latte"

So with cafés springing up everywhere, gas stations selling espresso in little paper cups, and latte a household word, Americans must be drinking more coffee than ever, right? Well, no, actually.

U.S. per-capita coffee consumption peaked at 3.12 cups per day in 1962, the year that the International Coffee Agreement was being negotiated. That was the glory year for Old Coffee: the industry that had built itself up from humble beginnings to become an international wheeler-and-dealer and America's champion against Communism in Latin America. Since then, U.S. per capita consumption has dwindled steadily to 1.64 cups per day in 2004.

Even with the success of the specialty sector, the U.S. coffee market today is growing only slightly. The dynamism it once displayed has moved on to Europe and Asia (particularly Japan, the world's sixth-largest consumer and home to 575 Starbucks outlets by 2005). China, with 218 Starbucks stores, looms large on the horizon. Nestlé, ever the leader among the multinational conglomerates, has several processing plants in Asia and a growing brand presence there as well. The United States, responsible for up to 80 percent of world consumption during World War II, now accounts for only 20 percent, and the EU is the largest coffee-drinking bloc.

Consumption has also grown in coffee-producing countries. After the United States, Brazil is now the second-largest consumer (there too, much to the horror of the coffee industry, the battle with soft drinks is beginning to rage). Interspersed among a number of European consumers, Indonesia is the fifth-largest and Mexico is the tenth.

And the ways in which those beans are being drunk is changing. In the United States, and increasingly abroad, the specialty coffee industry continues to grow, flooding the marketplace with all manner of choice and variety. No longer content to choose between regular and decaf, today's coffee drinker can essentially custom-order the drink, with choices at every stage of the formulation. Bean origin, processing, roast, grind, extraction method, concentration, adjuncts, sweeteners, and serving container are all negotiable at the average café, creating ever-advancing opportunities for pedantry and fetishism.

Today's coffee lover can choose coffee from distinctive regions in nearly fifty countries. Like wine, coffee is developing marks of origin, including Kona, Blue Mountain, Terrazu, Yergacheffe, Kalossi, and so on. Real devotees can even go for the ultimate cupping prize: Indonesian Luak (or Luwak), coffee that has been eaten off the bush by a civet and retrieved, still in its parchment, from the beast's droppings. For the luxury of having the fermentation stage of processing take place in a small mammal's gut, aficionados who appreciate its musky flavor can expect to pay $300 a pound. (This sort of thing is usually the province of the growing band of home roasters. Beginning in the 1990s with the small electric ovens used by the industry to test-roast samples, or even with popcorn poppers, their push for authenticity takes them back to the nineteenth century. But now they have a new generation of high-tech home-roasting gear and online access to the very best beans on the planet.)

As the specialty market develops and matures, it is passing out of a stage of no-holds-barred growth. Just as the coffee industry in general went through a period of questionable claims and qualities, the specialty coffee industry is experiencing consolidation and shakeout. In 1996, for example, a Kona scandal broke in which several prominent producers were found to be re-bagging cheaper Central American coffees and transshipping them through Hawai'i as Kona. This helped to explain how world Kona consumption has been, at times, up to ten times greater than Kona production.[7] In this overheated, affluent market, consumers had been willing to buy the more expensive "Kona" simply because it was more expensive. Ironically, the Central American beans substituted in this scam were generally recognized by professional cuppers as better tasting than real Kona.

In response to this problem, which culminated in federal charges for the perpetrators, the Kona Coffee Council and the Hawai'ian Coffee Association have begun to regulate the origin more closely. A parallel process has taken place in Jamaica, where the Blue Mountain origin had been similarly abused. Other producers, notably Guatemala, Costa Rica, and Colombia, are also developing systems of appellation, often bringing in wine experts to advise on their creation.

In a marked departure from the conventional commodity trade, with its lopsided access to market information that favors giant corporations and its single-minded focus on quantity over quality, today's trade in specialty coffee is based on a much more even flow of information between growers and traders. Better communication and feedback from importers, as well as targeted programs by international development organizations, like the Coffee Quality Institute and TechnoServe (which counts Jerry Baldwin, Starbucks founder and former head of Peet's, among its board members) and even some USAID programs, have been helping growers improve coffee quality.

Most coffee farmers have only a vague idea of how their product is consumed. The only signal they receive from their market is the fluctuating price, which has seemingly little to do with anything they have any control over. They receive no feedback on their cultivation and processing methods or techniques from their ultimate customers yet, just as much as roasting and brewing, cultivation and washing are crucial in ensuring that great beans result in a great cup. As a result, potentially sublime beans were disappearing into the wilderness of commodity coffee.

Quality improvement initiatives that educate farmers have resulted in a better supply of higher-quality beans. As well, they've turned some excellent coffees into near-perfect coffees, and are beginning to noticeably raise the quality of the coffee available to consumers. For those willing to seek it out, the best gourmet coffee has never been better.

These efforts have resulted directly in higher prices for farmers able to improve their quality. News of these high prices creates incentives for other coffee farmers to improve their crop. With a product good enough to be differentiated from the commodity stream, growers are less susceptible to the vagaries of the volatile market because the specialty industry will always pay a premium for excellent coffee. Conversely, when growers are barely even meeting their costs of production, as is all too often the case, they cannot afford to invest in maintenance and pest control. This downward quality spiral knocks them out of the running for true gourmet coffee—although not necessarily for mass specialty roasters.

Improved quality and the trend toward appellation signals the further gentrification of the specialty coffee industry. The three-dollar latte is clearly appealing to a different sector of society than the full pound of canned coffee that costs just a bit more.

As the gap in U.S. incomes widens, the distinction between specialty coffee and lower-priced mass-market coffee will continue to grow.

These changes in the marketplace have both influenced and been made possible by changes in the way specialty coffee is traded; increasingly, this market bears little relation to the commodity-coffee market. There are signs that the two sectors are on the verge of completely decoupling from one another. The economic challenges the industry faces are completely different from those faced by the Old Coffee sector: not enough top-quality beans rather than too many abominable beans. The nearing obsolescence of the New York "C" price in this market is a signal that the specialty sector is becoming unstuck from the mass-market coffee industry.

Toward that end, in recent years, some of the highest-end specialty coffee is being sold to traders and roasters via Internet auctions. There are three key specialty auctions: one run by the SCAA; another called the Q Auction, which is run by the Coffee Quality Institute and partly funded by USAID; and the Cup of Excellence, initiated by the ICO but managed today by the Alliance for Coffee Excellence. The auctions choose semifinalists within a particular country and make samples available to qualified bidders who then bid against one another online.

By connecting farmers directly with importers and roasters, the auctions have the dual benefit of helping traders identify and purchase the most hard-to-find top-quality beans, while returning a much higher purchase price to the producers. In a 2004 SCAA auction, traders paid an all-time Internet auction high of $21 per pound—about 2,000 percent higher than the "C" price in New York—for coffee from Hacienda La Esmeralda in Panama.

While this auction was for only seven bags of coffee—SCAA and Cup of Excellence are boutique auctions, selling only ten to twenty bags of coffee in each lot—the Q Auction sells container loads (250 bags) at a time. In the first two seasons since its 2004 launch, the Q Auction has helped sell 2 million pounds of gourmet cof-

U.S. Coffee Drinking by Age Group

Source: NCA

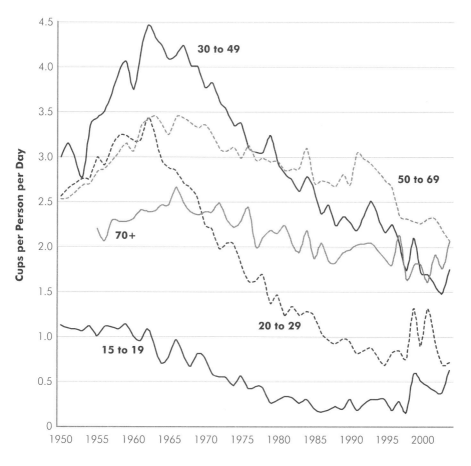

30 to 49

50 to 69

70+

20 to 29

15 to 19

Cups per Person per Day

Specialty coffee has transcended its role as breakfast beverage, and has become, for many, both art and lifestyle.

fee. In order to ensure that the benefits reach beyond the exporter, the Coffee Quality Institute requires that the farmers earn at least 75 percent of the sale price, and requests that they invest 2 percent of these revenues in local community-development projects.

The specialty industry tapped into an unfulfilled desire for diversity and quality among affluent coffee drinkers. In so doing, it has certainly stopped the slide in overall coffee consumption, and has even produced an increase for the first time in a third of a century—in 1998, just when specialty was really taking off, 5 million more Americans reported drinking coffee than in 1997, and almost half of all Americans reported drinking a specialty coffee drink in that year.[8] And the future looks brighter than it has for some time: while the overall American coffee market is relatively stagnant, the specialty industry grew by an average of 20 percent each year in the decade to 2004. Today, 16 percent of American adults (34 million of us) drink gourmet coffee daily—up from 9 percent in 1999—and more than half of adults drink it at least occasionally.[9]

The genius of coffee is that, regardless of the cultural, political, or health associations that damage its reputation in one period, it always comes back. It is fundamentally compelling to humankind, and no amount of mismanagement or neglect can prevent human beings from seeking out the simple, warming joy of a deep cup of the stuff. Currently in the Growth Phase of the product life cycle, specialty coffee is undergoing a rapid evolution as new products and business concepts constantly emerge amid a competitive but flourishing industry. While some of these concepts— Dunkin' Donuts' Dunkaccino, Red Hook's Coffee Beer, and Wolfgang Puck's self-heating coffee drinks, to name a few—should fall away deservedly quickly, others (including the dramatic rise of sustainably produced coffees) are transforming the very nature of the coffee trade, potentially going so far as to fundamentally reconfigure relationships still rooted in the not-so-distant colonial past.

6

The Sustainable
Coffee Buzz

Consumers have more control over the food chain than many of us think.
Since the free-market system respects buying power above all else, consumers
need to speak the language the market recognizes. That means expressing a
clear choice about how we want our food grown, processed, and delivered to us,
and whom we want to profit from the conduct of trade.

—Myrna Greenfield, *Making Coffee Strong* (1994)

MOST OF US GIVE LITTLE THOUGHT to the intricate system of trade and transport that brings us the food we eat. Where did those mid-winter raspberries come from? How did they get here? Which tropical country grew my bananas? How many miles did they travel to get here? Who picked my coffee beans, and what is that person's life like?

But the wave of change that specialty coffee rode during the nineties—a new acknowledgment of more subtle product qualities over and above mere inexpensiveness—set the stage for coffee to lead the charge into another emerging trend: embodying social change within the marketplace.

While sophisticated systems of processing and distribution move coffee and money from one country to another, they are poor at transmitting information. Because most coffee is traded as a commodity, any facts beyond the qualities of the beans themselves are considered extraneous by the conventional market. But with the advent of the specialty sector and increased interest on the part of consumers in where their coffee comes from, more information started to make it into the cup as well, and this soon became the basis for new ways of doing business.

Early Awakenings

Consciousness about the social and ecological dimensions of our consumption first emerged in the 1960s and 1970s with a series of interrelated milestones, including the publication of Rachel Carson's *Silent Spring* (1962), the passage of the Clean Air Act (1970), the first Earth Day (1970), the Clean Water Act (1972), and the growth of the farmworkers' movement and grape boycott of the 1970s.

Soon after, disasters like Love Canal (1978), Three Mile Island (1979), Bhopal (1984), and Chernobyl (1986), as well as mounting evidence against dioxin (through the 1970s and 1980s), triggered a healthy public skepticism about corporate and government accountability. Together, these developments laid the groundwork for a consumer movement that embraced natural, nonchemical living and was deeply suspicious of the established corporate order.

One of the most visible marketplace manifestations of this social change was slow but steady growth in demand for natural foods throughout the 1970s and 1980s. By the 1980s and early 1990s, natural food had become associated in the minds of an influential segment of the public with wholesome quality—the clean, crisp taste of apples from the tree. Part of the same wave that first brought specialty coffee to prominence, the sector began growing rapidly.

The idea that doing things differently for political reasons could lead to a better quality of life in the narrow terms of the marketplace was an eye-opener for many Americans, and it set the stage for a more sophisticated integration of cause and commerce. By the early 1990s, when media stories surfaced with heart-wrenching footage of absurdly poorly-paid and demoralized workers in Indonesian sweatshops producing $150 sneakers for Nike, many consumers were prompted to examine their buying habits more carefully.

After similar revelations about Kathie Lee Gifford's apparel line—found to be manufactured in Honduran sweatshops—and the ugly secrets behind a whole host of consumer favorites, including J. Crew, Tommy Hilfiger, the Limited, Guess?, Wal-Mart, and Disney, 84 percent of Americans said they would pay more for clothes made without the use of sweatshop or child labor.[1] Three quarters of Americans said they would switch brands or retailers to favor a company associated with a good cause.[2]

In 1999, show-stopping protests at the World Trade Organization meeting in Seattle announced to the world widespread opposition to the corporate version of globalization that had been proceeding unquestioned since the end of the Cold War. In a rare historical moment, advocacy groups from diverse causes—labor, the environment, and social justice—were united as one front against the global corporate domination of trade and the vision of commercial control of civil society that it implies. More and more people began to question the origins and contexts of their consumer goods, and the term "Fair Trade"—the idea that producers in less-developed countries should not be exploited—started to make intuitive sense to many.

A New Form of Food Activism

At the heart of this struggle is the question of what it means to be a "consumer." The word blatantly defines a person's social role as little more than a node on the receiving end of a commodity chain. It connotes a passivity that belies the fact that the "consumer," as the source of all of the money entering the chain, is in fact its driving member. But when the consumer awakens as a citizen and realizes that the products coming out of our society's trading infrastructure include not only running shoes, diamonds, and fine coffee, but also sweatshops, war, and devastation, the balance of power in the chain of commerce has suddenly shifted.

As mounting environmental and social problems began to hit people in developed countries where they live, an understanding of the interconnected nature of the global biosphere began to change buying practices. A ubiquitous product that comes from the other side of the world with relatively little processing, coffee was an early focus of food activism. Nestlé, Procter & Gamble, Kraft/Altria (formerly Philip Morris), and Starbucks have all endured boycotts of their coffee and public protests over their business practices. In each case, U.S. consumer groups took the company to task for its behavior yet, with the exception of Starbucks, innovative response has been sluggish.

Since 1977, Nestlé has been the target of a long-running boycott over its aggressive marketing of infant formula in developing countries (formula is more expensive and less nutritious than breast milk, and it needlessly exposes young children to

179

unsafe water supplies). Maxwell House and other Philip Morris products have been boycotted by groups outraged at the marketing of cigarettes around the world. Of the largest roasters, however, only P&G and Starbucks have suffered major consumer actions specifically over their coffee operations.

Some of the beans in Folgers, P&G's flagship coffee brand, are sourced from El Salvador. Throughout that country's history, the coffee plantation owners have been among the power elite, controlling politics and commerce with their vast landholdings and long-standing networks of influence. In the late 1980s and early 1990s, while the civil war in El Salvador was raging, all evidence pointed to the landowners' involvement in supporting death squads that were murdering activists, priests, opposition politicians, and civilians.

San Francisco-based nonprofit Neighbor to Neighbor and Jamie Gamble, the great-grandson of P&G's founder, targeted Folgers for a well-publicized boycott in the early 1990s. Among other outreach activities, they produced a shocking television commercial narrated by actor Ed Asner, whose voice-over charged Folgers with "brewing misery, destruction, and death" in El Salvador, while the video image showed blood pouring out of a coffee cup.

P&G's initial response was part and parcel of old-line coffee arrogance: the company pulled all of its advertising from stations that dared to air the Neighbor to Neighbor ad. But the activists managed to persuade several prominent supermarket and restaurant chains to give up Folgers, much to the alarm of P&G, which had been urged to stay in El Salvador by the U.S. State Department and the George H. W. Bush administration. Finally, just before the cease-fire in 1992, P&G teamed up with Kraft and Nestlé to buy ads in San Salvador newspapers in support of peace talks that were then taking place in New York.

When activists turned their attention to the new specialty industry, the response reflected the different culture of this sector. Starbucks has long prided itself on how it treats its employees—features like flexible schedules, health benefits even for part-timers, and, early on, a stock-options plan, were important pillars of the company's familial self-image. And with good reason: Starbucks has always had far less turnover than other retail and food-service companies. The company sees itself as a strongly positive community force.

While Starbucks had perhaps grown used to activists condemning it for being part of the chain-store invasion of once-distinctive neighborhoods, they were taken by surprise in 1994 by a new line of attack. When activists from the U.S./Guatemala Labor Education Project accused the corporation of being indifferent to the plight of farmers producing its raw materials—surely an important part of the Starbucks family—at first the company reacted angrily. Initially, Starbucks did little more than point to its corporate giving programs with CARE (to which it was the largest corporate donor), which runs literacy programs in coffee-producing regions.

But with its careful attention to the tastes of its customers, as well as the attitudes of its employees, the company quickly realized that mere denials were not enough—the very reputation of the young company was at stake among the people who mattered the most to it. This created an internal tension: a company that prided itself on doing the right thing for its "family" could not quite bring itself to fully face the accusations of its critics. In 1995 the company released a relatively weak set of "responsible" sourcing guidelines with little enforcement power, but that nonetheless served to diminish the momentum of the protest.

Five years later the situation had changed. In the midst of consolidating its coast-to-coast expansion, Starbucks had become far more visible—and was, for the first time, a billion-dollar company. And, this time, the activists had a clear-cut demand with a simple solution. A Fair Trade Certification label had been introduced for coffee in the United States, providing independent means to ensure that producers are treated fairly.

ITS GUATEMALAN :
ESPRESSO REPRESSO

In 1999, Global Exchange, a human rights organization that had been gaining recognition for its anti-sweatshop campaign against the Gap, launched a national campaign urging Starbucks to offer Fair Trade Certified coffee. In February 2000, after a TV news segment exposed child labor and scandalously low wages on Guatemalan farms that sold to Starbucks, Global Exchange organized a San Francisco protest. Subsequent news reports coupled footage of impoverished children picking coffee with images of protesters dumping lattes on the sidewalk. Global Exchange also went to the Starbucks shareholder meeting in Seattle, interrupting what the company had hoped would be a triumphant celebration of prosperity. Starbucks saw the seriousness of the potential PR debacle as nationwide protests at their stores loomed. In April, just before a major specialty coffee industry gathering in San Francisco, the company announced plans to offer a Fair Trade Blend in all their stores. Again, the protests were defused, and Starbucks spun the launch of its Fair Trade Blend as an act of unprovoked altruism. After the launch it was often far easier for customers to find pamphlets about the coffee than the blend itself.

This tactic was used once again when the Organic Consumers Association targeted Starbucks later in 2000, calling on the company to use more Fair Trade coffee, to use organic milk, and to pledge to eschew genetically modified coffee. Starbucks took to offering its customers organic milk, but only if they asked for it specifically.

Starbucks has been a recurring target for activists for several reasons. Coffee illuminates the inequities of global trade perfectly, and the company is the largest player by far in the high-profile specialty coffee sector. Not only does this make the company an ideal target in terms of publicity, but it also suggests that a campaign that brings about a change in Starbucks' practices could result in a real, meaningful difference—after all, this company alone buys 2 percent of all the coffee traded worldwide and 1 percent of America's milk, so changes in the way it operates could have huge repercussions. With its often fatal impact on small independent cafés, Starbucks also represents the kind of corporatized cultural imperialism that enrages activists, and punitive action can lead the company to think twice before moving into certain locations. Parts of San Francisco, for example, are no-go zones for Starbucks stores because the company judges the inevitable furor not to be worth it. Further, the company's ubiquity makes it easy to organize nationwide protests at company stores, especially for diffuse networks of Internet-connected activists. Finally, activists know that a publicly traded company like Starbucks, with an educated and largely socially responsible clientele, will be sensitive to public criticism about its human-rights record, and Nestlé's experience shows how hard it is to shake entrenched negative public impressions on this score.

But at its root is the fact that the humble coffee bean can embody so many of the problems in the world, bringing them into our daily lives whether we know it or not, as the authors of *Stuff: The Secret Life of Everyday Things* make vivid:

> The buzzing would not go away. Without opening my eyes, I hit the clock radio. My brain managed to hold one coherent thought: caffeine.
>
> I staggered into the kitchen to brew a cup of coffee. It took 100 beans—about one-sixtieth of the beans that grew on the coffee tree that year. The tree was on a small mountain farm in the Antioquia region of Colombia . . . Farmworkers wearing shorts, T-shirts, and sloshing backpacks sprayed my tree with several doses of pesticides synthesized in Germany's Rhine River Valley.
>
> Workers earning less than a dollar a day picked my coffee berries by hand and fed them into a diesel-powered crusher, which removed the beans from the pulpy berries that encased them. The pulp was dumped in the Cauca River. The beans, dried under the sun, traveled to New Orleans on a ship in a 132-pound bag. For each pound of beans, about two pounds of pulp had been dumped into the river . . . At New Orleans, the beans were roasted for 13 minutes at 400°F. The roaster burned natural gas pumped from the ground in Texas. The beans were packaged in four-layer bags constructed of polyethylene, nylon, aluminum, and polyester. They were trucked to a Seattle warehouse in an 18-wheeler, which got six miles per gallon of diesel. A smaller truck then took the roasted beans to my neighborhood store. Two hours after I finished my morning cup, my body had metabolized the coffee. Most of the water and some nutrients passed into the Seattle sewer system.
>
> I drink two cups a day. At that rate, I'll down 34 gallons of Java this year, made from 18 pounds of beans. The Colombian farms have 12 coffee trees growing to support my personal addiction. Farmers will apply 11 pounds of fertilizers and a few ounces of pesticides to the trees this year. And Colombia's rivers will swell with 43 pounds of coffee pulp stripped from my beans.[3]

Ethical Consumerism

But in the marketplace, no matter how embarrassing they may be, protests can only point the way to the real power: organized consumerism. Any company can add a single organic coffee to its product mix, getting on with business as usual while allowing activists to declare victory. But no company can ignore changing consumer preference for long—just ask the supermarket coffee roasters.

Since the 1990s, the organic market in the United States has grown by an average of 20 percent per year, five times faster than the food industry as a whole. In 2000 the National Organic Foods Standards Act marked the arrival of this once-fringe movement into the mainstream. Vigorous citizen involvement was crucial in ensuring that the act was free from egregious agribusiness concessions: in 1998 inadequate proposed standards precipitated a deluge of more than 280,000 letters of protest, more than the U.S. Department of Agriculture had ever received on a single issue before. Although some of its details remain controversial among the original organic pioneers, the uniform and credible standards for the use of the term "organic" that the act provides have greatly boosted public understanding and acceptance of the term. Indeed, the act has ultimately facilitated the adoption of organic certification by the largest food corporations. Though they had initially opposed the concept, they were won over by its profitability.

Most large multinational food brands now hold at least one organic line—including P&G, Kraft, Unilever, Hain Celestial, and Heinz. The Natural Marketing Institute's research indicates that 30 percent of American consumers (62 million households) purchase organic products, and that U.S. organic sales reached $10.9 billion in 2004.⁴ Half of all organic food is now sold at conventional supermarkets, and some industry experts expect the U.S. organic market to exceed $30 billion by 2007.⁵

In 2000, the sociologist and author Paul Ray identified a new breed of consumers he calls "Cultural Creatives" who make purchase decisions based on ecological and social values:

> Since the 1960s, 26 percent of the adults in the U.S.—50 million people—have made a comprehensive shift in their worldview, values, and way of life—their culture, in short. These creative, optimistic millions are at the leading edge of several kinds of cultural change, deeply affecting not only their own lives but our larger society as well. . . .
>
> The sheer size of the Cultural Creative population is already affecting the way Americans do business and politics. They are the drivers of the demand that we go beyond environmental regulation to real ecological sustainability, to change our entire way of life accordingly. They demand authenticity at home, in the stores, at work, and in politics. They support women's issues in many areas of life. They insist on seeing the big picture in news stories and ads. This is already influencing the marketplace and public life.⁶

This demographic values not only natural foods and socially responsible business; they also value (and make purchases relating to) personal development and alternative healthcare. According to Ray, Cultural Creatives represent a market worth $230 billion.

Obviously the best way for a company to reach this sought-after segment is by offering products that match its values. The general decommodification of coffee promoted by the specialty industry has helped create a constituency ready to hear the message of sustainable coffee—a constituency ready to put its money where its mouth is. And it has simultaneously created the means for doing so—an impossible notion in commodity coffee, which lacks the concept of differentiation and offers "quality" only as a simulacrum: a darker roast or whole beans that are just as insipid as ever. Although the early pioneers of social responsibility and organics brought their products to the marketplace before there was an overwhelming demand—using a "push" strategy in which supply engenders demand—today's Cultural Creatives have been a driving force in the development of a thriving ecologically and socially conscious marketplace.

In 2005, the Natural Marketing Institute reported that nine out of ten Americans say it is important for companies to look beyond pure profitability and to be mindful of their impact on the environment and society. The study also found that 70 percent of consumers say they are more likely to buy the products or services of companies that they believe are conscious of these issues.[7]

But the real measure of this movement is not what people say but what they do with their money. The Fair Trade Federation, an association of Fair Trade businesses, estimates that sales of Fair Trade products (including coffee, clothing, and handicrafts) in North America and the Pacific Rim reached $292 million in 2003—a 52-percent increase over 2002. Sales in 2004 were estimated at $376 million. According to the Social Investment Forum, investment funds that screen companies for their environmental and social impacts are now valued at more than $2.6 trillion.

The three primary commercial offshoots of what the industry terms "sustainable coffees" are organic, Fair Trade, and bird-friendly or shade coffee. Although each has a different focus, they all aim to create tangible benefits for coffee-growing regions by harnessing consumer choice. The fact that much overlap exists among the three—many organic coffees are also bird-friendly and many Fair Trade coffees are both organic and bird-friendly—means that the success of each furthers the objectives of the others. (Although they are different enough that efforts to create a "super label" have gone nowhere.) Now a vibrant sector with thousands of players, each seeking to distinguish itself from the next while cooperating on larger social goals, the sustainable coffee industry began as a niche within a niche. But as the specialty market has grown, coffee has become a pioneer in sustainability within the food industry—and even within consumer culture as a whole.

New Institutions: Third-Party Certification

Credibility in the marketplace is critical to the success of products that make claims about environmental and social benefits. Because organic, Fair Trade, and bird-friendly coffees sell themselves as being different from other beans in intangible attributes, there must be a way for consumers to verify the claims of companies selling their products as such. Otherwise, the entire sustainable coffee industry is open to the kind of fraud that has so damaged the reputation of Kona coffee.

The only tried-and-true way of ensuring that these claims are credible is through third-party certification—a centuries-old practice whereby an outside entity vouches for specific attributes of a product. In agricultural certification programs, an independent agency inspects the operations of a grower and determines whether or not they adhere to certain standards. The certifier's mark lets consumers be sure that the product is what the seller says it is. Historically, this kind of system has upheld things like the purity of precious metals and the quality of French wines. Today certification is the basis for the credibility of sustainable coffees.

Organic Coffee

Instead of using harmful agrichemicals like DDT, malathion, and benzene hexachloride—all commonly used in conventional coffee farming—organic coffee farming techniques focus on maintaining good soil quality and plant health as the most effective means of boosting productivity and immunity against disease. Toward that end, organic farmers often maintain a secondary shade crop over the coffee, weed with a machete, fertilize with compost, spread disease-resistant mulch, and introduce beneficial insects to eat pests. Such organic methods are much healthier for farmers, surrounding waterways, wildlife, and vegetation, and, many contend, result in better-tasting beans.

While the transition to organic practices can be relatively easy for smaller-scale farmers—many cannot afford expensive chemical inputs anyway—certification adds to their costs of production. However, because a typical organic coffee cooperative might have 250 to 300 small-scale growers, the fees are easily compensated for by the premium price for certified organic coffee—an average of 15 to 25 cents per pound.

The first certified organic coffee came to the United States in 1980, via Café Altura, a company based in Ojai, California. The company's owner, Chris Shepherd, was an organic food importer and exporter who had heard from a customer about the coffee from Finca Irlanda, an organic grower in Chiapas. Although he had no experience with it, his instincts told him that organic coffee could be big.

However, while the quality was high, Shepherd found it challenging to sell: not only was the specialty coffee industry anything but an "industry," but organic was still a relatively new concept. Worse, many health-food stores simply considered coffee to be bad for you and refused to carry it, organic or not. Nevertheless, Shepherd grew a small customer base spurred as much by the quality of Altura's coffee as its mission.

Altura was typical of the coffee companies that slowly built the organic coffee market in the 1980s and early 1990s: driven by charismatic individuals, many of these pioneers were located in the West, where ethical consumerism was beginning to take hold at a time when specialty coffee was still an alternative underground. These organic hardliners refused to be complicit in poisoning the very farmers and environment they depended on to produce excellent beans—people and places they had come to know personally in the course of building their businesses.

Connecting their core product with the real people and real landscapes they encountered in coffee-growing regions was transformative for many of the early proponents of organic. The inequities of the coffee trade were made clear to them, as was the possibility of creating a positive impact through their businesses. It also didn't hurt that in many cases the extra care taken by organic farmers, as well as the concomitantly better soil quality and plant health, could yield a distinctly better cup.

At a time when consumers at large were not yet clamoring for organics, these pioneering companies and their outstanding coffee played a vital role in educating the public (retailers, too) and demonstrating that high quality could go hand in hand with sustainability.

Some of the people behind the first companies to offer organic, such as Gary Talboy (Coffee Bean International; one of the founders of the Specialty Coffee Association of America), Paul Katzeff (Thanksgiving Coffee), and later, David

Organic Certification

Generally speaking, all natural substances are allowed in organic production and all synthetic substances are prohibited. Current guidelines also specifically prohibit the use of genetic engineering, ionizing radiation, and sewage sludge in organic production and handling.

The International Federation of Organic Agriculture Movements (IFOAM) is the umbrella organization that unites more than 750 member organizations (producers as well as certifiers) in over 100 countries. IFOAM unifies organic standards and verification practices and accredits certifiers, ensuring that organic certification means the same thing all over the world.

IFOAM also promotes the interests of the organic movement in international agricultural and environmental negotiations with the United Nations and multilateral institutions.

In the United States, USDA regulations stipulate that coffee must be certified by approved organizations like the Organic Crop Improvement Association (OCIA), Quality Assurance International (QAI), and Farm

Verified Organic. For coffee to carry the USDA organic label, it's not enough that the beans were grown on a certified organic farm; the importer and roaster must be certified organic as well.

Griswold (Aztec Harvest, and more recently Sustainable Harvest) have served leadership roles within the Specialty Coffee Association of America (SCAA), in turn influencing larger roasters and even non-specialty roasters hoping to cash in on the new sector.

In 1998, when the overall organic food market was beginning to explode, the SCAA coordinated a Sustainable Coffee conference in Denver. Beyond simply raising the profile of organics, the conference educated coffee businesses about the benefits and challenges of organics, helping it become the fastest-growing segment of their burgeoning industry. The SCAA went on to incorporate sustainability into its mission statement and make it an important theme in many subsequent events, propelling the concept further within coffee than had been done in most comparable industries.

Today, certified organic coffee accounts for about 5 percent of specialty sales, and more than half of all U.S. specialty firms sell it.[8] According to the National Coffee Association—which, tellingly, now tracks sustainable coffee in its National Coffee Drinking Trends Report—half of daily coffee drinkers are aware of organic coffee, although only a quarter of those aware of it have actually purchased it.[9] The trend shows no sign of slowing: organic coffee sales increased by about 40 percent in natural food stores and doubled in conventional supermarkets in 2005.[10]

Shade or Bird-Friendly Coffee

In the mid-1990s, biologists discovered a marked decline in populations of tropical migratory songbirds—birds like orioles and warblers that winter in the shaded, forest-like habitat of traditional coffee farms in Latin America. Further investigations revealed that the declines were linked to the trend in coffee technification, which uses modernized varieties that prefer full sun, requiring the removal of traditional shade trees and the use of additional chemicals. Throughout the 1970s and 1980s, vast areas of traditional coffee farms in Latin America had been technified, destroying critical habitat for the songbirds. Significantly, U.S. consumers could personally see the disappearance of the beloved songbirds from their own backyards and relate it to their coffee-drinking habit—a connection that was publicized by birding organizations like the American Birding Association and the Audubon Society.

In 1996, the Smithsonian Migratory Bird Center (SMBC), which had conducted some of this early research, sponsored the first major conference focused on sustainability in the coffee industry. The conference stimulated the SMBC to develop standards and a labeling scheme for shade-grown, "bird-friendly" coffee from traditional farms. In a country of some 70 million birdwatchers, it's not surprising that shade coffee became very popular and helped expand consumer awareness for the concept of sustainable coffee among specialty coffee drinkers. The growth of shade coffee in the late 1990s represented a significant development in coffee-related activism. Unlike organic coffee, whose primary market driver is drinkers' personal health concerns about agrichemicals and not workers or the environment, the motivation to buy shade

Shade/Bird-friendly Certification

Today, there are two certification systems for shade coffee in the United States: one overseen by the Smithsonian Migratory Bird Center (SMBC), a nonprofit organization that conducts research and education about tropical migratory songbirds, and one coordinated through the Rainforest Alliance, a New York City-based nonprofit.

With standards based on scientific fieldwork, the SMBC's "Bird-Friendly" certification requires coffee farms to include a minimum of ten native tree species, have a minimum shade coverage of 40 percent of the land, and feature vertical structural diversity among the shade trees—elements that mimic the birds' natural habitat. Organic certification is required for SMBC certification, and many of the organic certifiers perform both annual inspections, paid for by the producer. Coffee companies in the United States pay the SMBC 25 cents per pound sold under their label.

The Rainforest Alliance certifies coffee, bananas, citrus, chocolate, cut flowers, and ferns. Although they aim to minimize environmental degradation and include some general labor standards, some in the industry criticize them for having criteria that are not strict enough to make a major impact. Unlike the SMBC, the Rainforest Alliance does not require their coffee to be organic, and their labor standards merely uphold minimum-wage laws in producing countries, which in some cases means less than $2 per day. Because they have looser standards, more farms—particularly large plantations—can qualify for their certification. And because the Rainforest Alliance program requires licensing fees only from producers, not roasters, it has been relatively successful in attracting big industry players like Kraft, Procter & Gamble, and Chiquita.

Having two different shade labels in the market, with different standards contributes to confusion in ways that adversely impact both efforts. Further, there is no global organization setting the certification standards for this cause as there is for Fair Trade and organic.

coffee is purely environmental. Rather than boycotting or protesting a company, consumers could support a cause simply by buying an alternative product.

In 2004, close to 100 million pounds of green coffee were certified shade-grown worldwide—95 percent by Rainforest Alliance and the rest by the SMBC. While the volume is relatively large, not all of it is marketed as such, and only 15 percent of American daily coffee drinkers are aware of shade-grown coffee.[11]

Fair Trade Coffee

Fair Trade focuses on the other element of coffee production that has darkened the cup for hundreds of years: exploitative working conditions. Unlike environmental externalities, labor is actually embodied in a product. So the focus of Fair Trade is to reconfigure the coffee value chain to put more, not less, of it into the hands of growers. The goal is to pay producers in developing countries enough so that their lives are not dead-end, marginal struggles. For an industry to be sustainable, it can't destroy the lives of the people who actually create the product.

In contrast to charity or aid, Fair Trade is a market-driven model that redefines the dynamics of the trading system to achieve this goal. Fair Trade relationships are simplified; exploitative middlemen are bypassed as farmer co-ops trade directly with importers in consuming countries. And, crucially, power across the value chain is equalized as growers have access to better market information and credit on fairer terms.

Reducing poverty in developing countries has long been a goal of governments,

Fair Trade Certification

Since 1997, Fairtrade Labeling Organizations International (FLO) has been the international standard-setting and certification organization for Fair Trade. The system that FLO developed was jump-started by coffee but has expanded to include tea, chocolate, bananas, mangoes, pineapples, sugar, rice, cut flowers, and more.

Through its regional offices in producing countries, FLO certifies producer groups and conducts annual inspections to ensure that they adhere to internationally-accepted Fair Trade criteria, which for coffee include worker-owned democratically-managed cooperatives, transparent administration, and investment in social development projects. After passing the inspection, producers are required to submit Fair Trade sales data to FLO each year detailing the volume, price paid, and buyers involved. With headquarters in Bonn, Germany, FLO works with Fair Trade labeling initiatives in twenty countries all over the world. These include all the biggest coffee consumers in Europe, North America, Japan, Australia, and New Zealand, as well as Mexico, which is also a major producer.

National labeling initiatives like TransFair USA certify and promote Fair Trade products once they enter consuming countries. In the United States, importers who want to sell Fair Trade Certified coffee sign an agreement with TransFair USA that specifies that they will trade on FLO's Fair Trade terms. This entails paying a minimum floor price of $1.26 per pound of green coffee, with an additional 15 cent premium if it is also certified organic. In rare cases when the world coffee price rises above this floor price, importers pay Fair Trade cooperatives a minimum of 5 cents per pound more than the prevailing price.

Roasters pay TransFair a volume-based fee to use the "Fair Trade Certified" label on each pound of coffee they sell. Licensed companies are required to submit quarterly reports detailing their purchases and sales of Fair Trade Certified products, allowing TransFair to audit the paper trail all the way back to the grower cooperative.

development agencies, nongovernmental organizations, and even many religious groups—indeed, coffee had been explicitly pressed into this role by the International Coffee Agreement of 1962. But the focus on governments and large roasters as agents of change had mixed results for farmers.

Fair Trade efforts to link producers and consumers directly date back to the 1940s, when groups in Europe and North America began importing handicrafts at prices higher than those provided through conventional trade.

In the early 1970s, the first Fair Trade coffee—Indio Solidarity Coffee—was imported directly from cooperative farms in Guatemala to Europe. But it was not until the late 1980s, amid falling world coffee prices, that a group in the Netherlands conceived of a labeling scheme that would distinguish fairly traded coffee from conventionally traded coffee. Named after the eponymous protagonist of an influential Dutch novel from the nineteenth century who protested the exploitation of colonial coffee plantation workers in Java, the "Max Havelaar" label guaranteed that producers had been provided Fair Trade terms.

In many regions, paying producers a fair price for their coffee means eliminating the middlemen, nicknamed "coyotes" in Central America for their vicious predatorial approach to coffee farmers mired in debt. Made up of small-scale family farmers, Fair Trade coffee cooperatives bypass the coyotes by selling directly to importers in consuming nations. In addition to guaranteeing a fair price for green coffee and engaging in transparent, long-term trading relationships, importers also agree to provide at least partial financing if needed. Importers also give feedback on coffee quality and best processing practices to the cooperatives, with the intention of helping them improve their businesses. The cooperatives invest part of their Fair Trade income in social development projects that benefit the local community—typically things like building schools, improving health care, restoring degraded land, diversifying crops, and developing infrastructure projects. Many cooperatives also invest part of their

Fair Trade: A Testimonial[12]

by Pedro Pablo Valenzuela,
CECOCAFEN co-op member, 2005

Thanks to Fair Trade, I still own plots of land to farm my coffee . . . If I sold my coffee at the market price, as my neighbors do, I would only be able to pay for food and other necessities. Fair Trade has allowed me to support my family, attend to health problems, and send my children to school, which is invaluable because I never had the opportunity.

The coffee that we produce is shade-grown, high-quality, and organic, which benefits our health as well as that of the animals in the habitat. Birds come and go with the seasons, and animals that were at the point of disappearing now live among us on the coffee farms. If I was not part of a cooperative or if we were not members of CECO-CAFEN, I would be telling you another story, like the many stories of my friends and neighbors who have had to travel to other areas and even other countries to be able to survive the terrible Coffee Crisis.

For a farmer like me, Fair Trade is a fundamental pillar of life.

income in quality improvement projects, which in turn helps them sell more of their coffee at better prices.

Fair Trade coffee in the United States got its start in 1986, with a coffee company called Equal Exchange. Much like the organic pioneers, Equal Exchange played a crucial role in introducing coffee drinkers and retailers to the Fair Trade concept before it became more generally known. Their outreach—which still includes building support among grassroots organizations, hosting farmer visits that allow farmers to share personal testimonies on the impact of Fair Trade, and bringing retailers to coffee farms—has significantly expanded the audience for Fair Trade beyond the predictable natural food audiences. In particular, the company has had notable success with religious groups.

"Would you like to come up for some willful exploitation of third world coffee farmers?"

Source: Equal Exchange

Based in Massachusetts but with distribution throughout the country, Equal Exchange remains the largest 100-percent Fair Trade coffee company in the country today (and one of the largest worker-owned cooperatives). Experiencing dramatic growth in recent years—20 to 30 percent per year, and $20 million in sales for 2005—Equal Exchange, perhaps better than any other company, is a living demonstration that a company can do well by doing good in the world. Indeed, Equal Exchange's approach has gained so much trust among coffee growers that a pair of Latin American Fair Trade producer co-ops have actually made substantial investments in the company.

Third-party Fair Trade certification did not begin in the United States until 1999, with the launch of TransFair USA. The organization's label became the focal point for companies like Equal Exchange, grassroots organizations, social justice activists, students, and religious groups that shared a common mission to alleviate poverty in developing countries. Some of these, like Global Exchange and Oxfam, went on to start their own Fair Trade campaigns that continue to this day. Fair Trade coffee was an appealing way to directly involve constituents in global issues: you could contribute to the cause through the simple act of choosing the right kind of coffee. In this way, it stood out from so many other social justice causes, which have focused on boycotts or protests, by giving people a way to take positive action in the course of their daily lives.

The emergence of a clearly defined path for roasters to address producer issues came at precisely the right time. The Coffee Crisis was just beginning, and many roasters were hearing horror stories of lost farms and devastated families from their suppliers. Genuine concern within the specialty sector, plus the constant search for ways to differentiate the sector from the old coffee industry, led to the rapid embrace of Fair Trade Certification by a number of smaller roasters. In 2000, just a year after TransFair launched, the SCAA officially endorsed the Fair Trade model as an effective way of helping coffee producers. They went on to make sustainability a core theme of that year's annual trade show in San Francisco, lending crucial institutional support to the concept.

Simultaneously, Starbucks launched its Fair Trade Blend. In spite of the fact that the company had been pressured into doing so by Global Exchange, Starbucks' Fair Trade launch signaled to the rest of the industry that Fair Trade could be integrated into the largest specialty coffee operations. And it radically changed the Fair Trade landscape: thanks to its sheer size, Starbucks quickly became almost as large a Fair Trade roaster as Equal Exchange, and eventually surpassed them in volume (although Fair Trade accounts for less than 5 percent of their total volume).

Initially, many specialty roasters were leery of Fair Trade coffee because they perceived quality could sometimes be uneven. Also, at first some of these co-ops suffered from a lack of information from their customers—a common problem for small-scale producers. But as Fair Trade grew, this changed quickly. Increased income and better communication with importers helped farmers invest in improvements that enhanced the quality of their coffee. Now, TransFair brings more than a hundred producers to its Fair Trade mega-booth at the SCAA trade show each year—a rare opportunity for farmers to attend quality-related presentations, participate in hands-on cupping workshops, meet customers, and even see their product on grocery store shelves. As well, in the true spirit of Fair Trade's goal of fostering long-term trading relationships, some roasters have become directly involved in helping cooperatives improve their quality.

Thanksgiving Coffee, for example, has teamed with USAID to build a cupping lab for producers in Nicaragua. Not only does this allow growers—many of whom had never tasted their own finished product—to judge their coffee the same way buyers do, but it allows them to do so alongside coffee samples from all over the world. Thanksgiving has even brought East African growers to this Central American facility in order to spread the knowledge further. In the process, the Fair Trade network's efforts have become an integral part of the overall specialty industry's push for quality in the past few years.

While the early endorsement of the SCAA and the participation of Starbucks helped build credibility on the quality front, Peet's launch of a Fair Trade blend in 2000 definitely signalled to the industry that Fair Trade coffees could be among the best. Highly regarded for its obsession with quality beans, Peet's had initially held back from Fair Trade for this reason. Once the company acknowledged that quality had improved, no practical objections remained for Fair Trade among most specialty roasters.

The impact of Fair Trade on farmers was never more poignant than during the devastating Coffee Crisis of 2001–2003, when coffee prices dropped to their lowest level ever, in real terms. At a time when global prices hovered near the low of 42 cents per pound many farmers were earning less than half of this. Earning $1.26 per pound for their green coffee (and $1.41 if it was certified organic), the Fair Trade co-ops were able to pay member farmers double and often triple the meager income that the conventional trade offered. During the Coffee Crisis, Fair Trade proved to be the best on-the-ground alternative, enabling farmers to maintain their way of life, keep their kids in school, and improve their crops.

In 2002 consumers sipped coffee at their kitchen tables, reading stories in the paper that included descriptions like this, from the *Wall Street Journal*:

> "We've had no work since February and are here begging for our lives," says Mr. Luna, a listless 33-year-old [former coffee farmer in Nicaragua], surrounded by a group of visibly malnourished, unshod children. They are living on wild bananas and the charity of passersby. "At least during the war there was food," he says.[13]

Coverage of the crisis served to humanize coffee for many and created a stronger link between consumers and producers, in turn fueling the rise in both consumer and industry interest in Fair Trade.

Still, reservations about Fair Trade came from several quarters: free marketeers derided Fair Trade as market interference; large coffee companies were unhappy that it did not extend to the large plantations they did business with; others were uncomfortable with the idea of reporting sales figures to what they saw as a radical movement; still others were afraid that carrying one Fair Trade coffee would imply the company's other offerings were unfairly traded; elites in some producing countries distrusted the political empowerment of rural people; and the activist tendency to place politics over flavor made the quality issue persist longer than it had to. But the fact remains that throughout the Coffee Crisis, while industry, aid groups, and governments were wringing their hands about what to do, Fair Trade was the only mechanism whereby small family farmers could help themselves simply by being farmers.

Today, more than 300 U.S. roasters offer Fair Trade Certified coffee, and it can be found in more than 35,000 retail stores in the United States, including impeccably mainstream outlets like Sam's Club, Costco, and Target. In late 2005, McDonald's announced plans to launch Fair Trade organic coffee in 650 New England locations.

Approximately 800,000 people at 221 co-ops in 25 countries sell more than 75 million pounds of green coffee each year through the global Fair Trade network. Still, this amounts to less than a third of the coffee these co-ops produce—the rest is sold in the conventional market at lower prices.

While the majority of co-ops in the Fair Trade register are basic at best, some of the more established ones like COOCAFE in Costa Rica and CECOCAFEN in Nicaragua are large concerns that now rival traditional traders in size and sophistication. Complete with amenities like staff agronomists, websites, and cupping labs, these few are proof that the Fair Trade approach can result in genuine rural development, and can do so without the inequities that often accompany agricultural development.

Worldwide Fair Trade sales in 2004 were $376 million,[14] putting it in the league of aid budgets from countries like Austria and Greece. Coffee is the single largest Fair Trade product, accounting for over 30 percent of total sales.

TransFair USA estimates that in 2004 farmers received $26 million in *additional* income (beyond what they would have earned on conventional terms) for the 33 million pounds of Fair Trade Certified coffee sold in the United States that year. This did more than merely help them get by: it improved their lives and the lives of their communities, all the while improving quality, and at little or no extra cost to coffee drinkers.

Going Mainstream

But if the rationale for sustainable coffee was starting to make sense to many in the specialty industry, in 1994 the old guard was perplexed:

> "Shade coffee?" asks George Boecklin, president [at the time] of the National Coffee Association, in New York. . . . "Coffee companies don't buy shade coffee or sun coffee or any particular thing. It's all about maintaining a consistent taste profile. Taste is the key". . . Andrea Cook of Nestlé Beverage's San Francisco office had never heard of the shade/sun coffee issue. "Price and quality are our two determinants," she says. "We have no relationship with the growers."[15]

More than a decade later, as their market share continues to slide, the majors are bringing up the rear and starting to reconsider.

Just as the largest roasters eventually responded to changing tastes by launching somewhat better quality coffees to great fanfare, they are now experimenting with sustainable coffees that seem to take up more space on press releases than store shelves. Nowadays, Procter & Gamble's "gourmet" Millstone line includes one Fair Trade Certified coffee and a Rainforest Alliance coffee—although, until recently, these coffees were only available online. Dunkin' Donuts offers espresso made from Fair Trade Certified beans, but did not advertise it as such in stores for close to three years, nor did it promote the fact anywhere other than on its website and in its initial press release. Kraft/Philip Morris (Altria) now blends Rainforest Alliance–certified coffee in some of their European brands and offers a 100-percent Rainforest Alliance blend in the UK and the United States—but just for food-service operations like hotels, restaurants, and cafeterias. Most recently, in late 2005, Nestlé launched a Fair Trade Certified canned instant coffee—but only in the UK. In other words, although it's easy to find PR from the majors about sustainable coffees, they are not widely advertised or even all that available: actually finding them and drinking them is something of a challenge.

Some of the larger corporations have sidestepped established sustainability labels entirely, instead developing self-regulated codes of conduct.

In 1997 Dutch retail giant Ahold launched the Utz Kapeh Code of Conduct, a third-party certification program that was originally designed to monitor product safety. Minimal environmental and labor standards were added to Utz Kapeh to take advantage of the burgeoning sustainable coffee market in Europe, and the label has been adopted by some big players, including Sara Lee/Douwe Egbert and Mitsui.

The Common Code of Conduct for the Coffee sector (known as 4C) is the product of a consortium of key players that includes farmers, importers, roasters (includ-

Growth of Fair Trade Certified Coffee in the U.S.

Source: TransFair USA

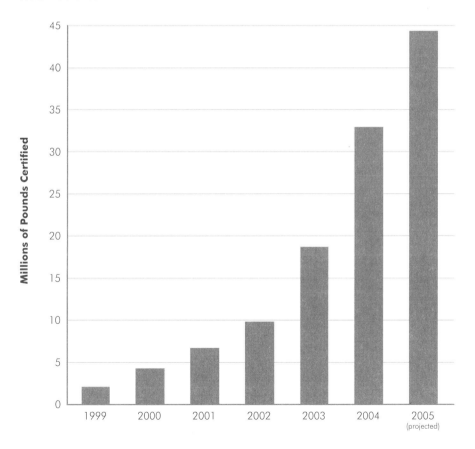

ing Nestlé, Kraft, and Sara Lee), NGOs, and trade unions. The self-enforced code prohibits the "worst forms" of child labor, slavery, the use of certain pesticides, cutting down forests in national parks, failure to provide legally required housing and drinking water to workers, and affirms the right of plantation workers to unionize.

An attempt to assert control over sustainability standards on their own terms, ultimately these codes of conduct come across about as genuine as caramel-flavored instant cappuccino.

At the other end of the spectrum, the mainstreaming of sustainability in coffee has alienated some of the true believers. Some of the same activists and visionary companies who helped launch the movement have grown to resent the growing number of companies who blatantly milk their meager Fair Trade offerings for public relations points. The pioneers, particularly companies that exclusively sell sustainable coffees, say such efforts amount to "fairwashing." In 2004, this tension led to several roasters dropping the Fair Trade Certified label from their packages, although they continue to use Fair Trade coffees and pay Fair Trade prices.

Starbucks is somewhere in the middle. The company has limited, though widely promoted, sustainable offerings, but it also has its own code of conduct. Although it now offers two organic coffees in its stores, it still sells only one Fair Trade product (responding to student activism on college campuses, its food-service division now offers several Fair Trade coffees). Nonetheless, Starbucks managed to sell 5 million pounds of Fair Trade Certified coffee in 2004, creating a tremendous impact on coffee communities. It projects twice that volume for 2005, making it the largest roaster of Fair Trade coffee in the country. Because of the company's reach, in many countries (including a number of coffee producers), Starbucks is the only Fair Trade coffee on the market.

Evolving from the original mid-1990s code of conduct that the company promulgated in response to activist concerns about labor practices in Guatemala, today's

Coffee and Farmer Equity (CAFE) practices is a set of sourcing guidelines that Starbucks applied to 43.5 million pounds of coffee purchased from preferred suppliers in 2004. Beyond the CAFE practices, and its Fair Trade, organic, and shade coffees, the company has also recently opened a Farmer Support Center in Costa Rica to provide technical assistance to farmers and formed an alliance with USAID and Conservation International to support conservation coffee projects in Latin America.

Starbucks' tactic of partially acceding to activists' demands—or, to put it more charitably, listening to activist concerns as important feedback about its performance—is dramatically different from the no-negotiation policy of Old Coffee. It arises from a larger contradiction that evolved from the dawn of consumer consciousness in the 1970s. Companies like Starbucks, Cascadian Farms, Ben & Jerry's, and Stonyfield Farms are now giant corporations, yet they are attempting to embody values whose philosophical underpinnings question the very legitimacy of the corporate model. Their customers love their products, yet many are also driven by a sense of social responsibility that demands much more from the companies they admit into their lives.

Are these companies nothing more than the same old corporate structure aping the style and rhetoric, but not the substance, of a co-opted movement? Or is this the movement itself taking over the means of commerce? At a deeper level, the fights over things like Fair Trade and organics are struggles about the meaning of business. You can now get a Fair Trade and completely organic café au lait at Starbucks, but only if you won't take no for an answer from the baristas. If a company like Starbucks has managed to have it both ways so far—it has found a way to be responsive without making radical changes—it is because this struggle has not yet been resolved within the company, the industry, or our society.

Out of the Murky Depths

Ultimately, substantial engagement by major players in the coffee value chain will be the only sustainable solution to the abuses of land and labor perpetrated in the name of the coffee consumer—of all consumers, for that matter.

In a globalized marketplace, our relationships with producers frequently extend to regions well beyond our political reach. When coffee was grown in actual colonies, home-country citizens could at least influence colonial administrations through domestic political processes, a minimal safeguard that curbed some of the worst excesses—including slavery in British colonies and forced labor on Dutch planta-tions—even at the height of the European colonial period. But under today's system of transnational exploitation, citizens have become consumers, with less recourse to political means of influencing conditions where the products we buy are made.

Fair Trade, organic, and bird-friendly certifications fill this void by providing a means to make policy in the absence of government channels. In an age of privatiza-tion, these initiatives privatize foreign policy and put it on the grocery store shelf. Although sometimes disparaged as interfering with "free markets," Fair Trade in par-ticular is actually a pure expression of free-market principles: in the absence of gov-ernment, Fair Trade commodifies policy and allows consumers to make a political choice with their purchase: policy is transformed into product.

Sustainable coffee at least partially covers territory that agencies like the ICO and World Bank once trod. But it is doing it on its own terms, on a person-to-person level. Sustainable coffee goes beyond just the decommodification of the bean. It's also a decommodification of producer and consumer, a way to understand that at each end of the international value chain there are living people. In a world where

The majority of specialty coffee roasters now offers Fair Trade, Organic, and/or Bird Friendly coffee, putting coffee at the forefront of the "sustainable" food movement, and creating a sometimes bewildering array of choice for coffee drinkers.

1 cent added to the price of a $3 latte could, if it made its way all the way up the value chain, double the income of the farmer who grew the coffee, Fair Trade is personalized globalization that reflects the values of coffee drinkers thankful for this magical black elixir.

By using market channels to effect social and ecological goals, sustainable coffee changes the role of the company providing these goods to a partnership with both producers and consumers. It is a glimpse of an economic system that is more harmonious with social and biological reality, yet still provides the best-quality product in an efficient manner. In this new arrangement, growers, traders, and drinkers are united in a vast project to enjoy delicious coffee and a better life for everyone—really, a grassroots version of the ambitious, top-down coffee trading agreements of the 1960s. The difference is that this one has the interests of consumers and producers—not only traders—at its heart.

It's not too much to say that the growing sustainable coffee sector is a bright spot in the overall grim picture of global trade: the shining light in the murky depths of your mug. This is one addiction we can feel good about.

Notes, Bibliography, and Image Credits

Notes

CHAPTER I: A BRIEF HISTORY OF COFFEE

1   Antoine Galland, *Lettre sur l'Origine et le Progres du Café* (Paris, 1699). Quoted in W. H. Ukers, *All About Coffee* (New York: The Tea and Coffee Trade Journal Company, 1935; republished by Gale Research Company, Book Tower, 1976), 8.

2   Leonhard Rauwolf, *Aigentliche beschreibung der Raisis so er vor diser zeit gegen auffgang inn die morgenlaender vilbracht* (Lauwingen, 1582–83). Quoted in Ukers, *All About Coffee*, 21.

3   Sheik Ansari Djezeri Hanball Abd-al-Kadir, 1587. Quoted in Heinrich Eduard Jacob, *Coffee, the Epic of a Commodity*, trans. Eden and Cedar Paul (New York: The Viking Press, 1935), 18.

4   Quoted in Jacob, *Coffee*, 116.

5   Ukers, *All About Coffee*, 24.

6   Richard Bradley, *The Virtue and Use of Coffee, with Regard to the Plague, and Other Infectious Distempers* (London: printed by E. Mathews and W. Mears, 1721), 24.

7   *Publick Adviser*, May 19–26, 1657. Quoted in Arthur Gray, *Over the Black Coffee* (New York: The Baker and Taylor Company), 1902.

8   Wolfgang Schivelbusch, *Tastes of Paradise: A Social History of Spices, Stimulants, and Intoxicants* (New York: Pantheon Books, 1992).

9   Michelet, *La Régence*. Quoted in Ukers, *All About Coffee*, 95.

10   Benjamin Moseley, *Treatise Concerning the Properties and Effects of Coffee* (London: printed for the author, and sold by John Stockdale opposite Burlington House, Piccadilly, 1785), 41–42.

11   Steve Bradshaw, *Café Society: Bohemian Life from Swift to Bob Dylan* (London: Wiedenfeld and Nicolson, 1978), 10.

12   Edward Forbes Robinson, *The Early History of Coffee Houses in England* (London: Kegan Paul, Trench, Trüber & Co, Ltd., 1893), 109.

13   Jacob, *Coffee*, 97.

14   Ralph Nevill, *London Clubs: Their History and Treasures* (London: Chatto and Windus, 1911), 2.

15   Isaac D'Israeli, *Curiosities of Literature* (London, 1824). Quoted in Norman Kolpas, *Coffee* (London: John Murray Pubs, 1977), 30.

16   Ukers, *All About Coffee*, 15.

17 *A Cup of Coffee: or, Coffee in Its Colours*, 1663. Quoted in Robinson, *Early History of Coffee Houses in England*, 112.

18 *The Women's Petition Against Coffee*, London, 1674.

19 *The Men's Answer to the Women's Petition Against Coffee*, London, 1674.

20 Quoted in Ukers, *All About Coffee*, 68.

21 Quoted in Jacob, *Coffee*, 49.

22 Quoted in Ukers, *All About Coffee*, 715.

23 Quoted in ibid., 42.

24 Elector of Cologne, Maximilian Frederick, Bishop of Munster, Duchy of Westphalia, *Manifesto of February 17, 1784*.

25 Jean Baptiste Tavernier, *Les six voyages de Jean Baptiste Tavernier . . . , qu'il a fait en Turquie, en Perse, et aux Indes . . .* (Paris, 1676). Quoted in Ulla Heise, *Coffee and Coffee Houses*, trans. Paul Roper (Pennsylvania: Schiffer Publishing Ltd., 1987).

CHAPTER 2: COFFEE'S ODYSSEY FROM CROP TO CUP

1 The oft-cited "second most valuable item of international trade" from the first edition of this book is no longer true, thanks to falling coffee prices and climbing prices for other commodities.

2 Tom Barry, *Roots of Rebellion* (Boston: South End Press, 1987), 27.

3 Ibid.

4 Patrick Pelini, "Putting a Face to Coffee: Part One," *North Country News* 16, no. 3 (March 1996).

5 Luis Hernandez Navarro, "Coffee: A Virtual Fiefdom," in *Proceedings of the First Sustainable Coffee Congress*, ed. R. A. Rice, A. M. Harris, and J. McLean (Washington, DC: Smithsonian Migratory Bird Center, 1997), 95.

6 Smithsonian Migratory Bird Center, *Why Migratory Birds Are Crazy for Coffee* (Washington, DC: Smithsonian Migratory Bird Center, 1997).

7 Andrés C. Uribe, *Brown Gold: The Amazing Story of Coffee* (New York: Random House, 1954), 92–94.

CHAPTER 3: THE RISE OF THE INTERNATIONAL COFFEE TRADE

1 Stavitsky, as quoted in Robert H. Bates, *Open-Economy Politics: The Political Economy of the World Coffee Trade* (Princeton: Princeton University Press, 1997), 126.

2 *Congressional Record*, May 20, 1963, 8552.

3 North London Haslemere Group, *Coffee: The Rules of Neocolonialism* (London: Third World First, 1972), 5.

4 Pan-American Coffee Bureau, *U.S. and the International Coffee Agreement*, 1964.

5 Joseph Short, *American Business and Foreign Policy: Cases in Coffee and Cocoa Trade Regulation 1961–1974* (New York: Garland Publishing Inc., 1987), 151–52.

6 Interviewed by Joseph Short, as quoted in ibid., 153–54.

7 Bates, *Open-Economy Politics*, 153.

8 Begun as a consortium of smaller roasters to compete with the instant coffees of the conglomerates, Tenco was bought by Minute Maid, which was in turn acquired by Coca-Cola in 1960.

9 Charles Meono, ed., *Coffee & Tea Industries*, February 1962, 28.

10 International Coffee Agreement, 1968.

11 North London Haslemere Group, *Coffee*, 16.

12 Another standout was OPEC, which is more like the earlier coffee agreements in that consumers do not participate. However, OPEC is a different beast because it does not struggle with variable harvests—oil output can be controlled precisely and inexpensively.

13 Rob Collier, "Mourning Coffee," *San Francisco Chronicle*, May 20, 2001.

14 John M. Talbot, "Where Does Your Coffee Dollar Go?: The Division of Income and Surplus along the Coffee Commodity Chain," *Studies in Comparative International Development* 32, no. 1 (1997): 56–91, 78–79.

15 Ibid., 78–79.

CHAPTER 4: HEALTH, MARKETING, AND THE MEGA-ROASTERS

1 Consumers Union of United States, Inc., "Coffee and Health." *Consumer Reports*. October, 1994.

2 A. Svilaas, "Intakes of Antioxidants in Coffee, Wine, and Vegetables are Correlated with Plasma Carotenoids in Humans," *Journal of Nutrition* 134 (2004): 562–67.

3 Terence McKenna, *Food of the Gods* (New York: Bantam Books, 1992), 184–85.

4 Atlantic Marketing Research survey sponsored by Seattle's Best Coffee, May 1998.

5 Oscar Schisgall, *Eyes on Tomorrow: The Evolution of Procter & Gamble* (New York: J. G. Ferguson Publishing Company, 1981), 230.

6 Editorial, "Coffee and Chemistry," *Coffee & Tea Industries*, July 1962, 39–40.

7   Alecia Swasy, *Soap Opera: The Inside Story of Procter & Gamble* (New York: Times Books, 1993), 117–18.

8   Ibid., 163–64.

9   Even in the offices of the National Coffee Association; while we interviewed Robert Nelson, its president, we enjoyed a cup of drip java and he sipped a Coke.

10 W. A. Heyman, "Why Not? Coffee as a Soft Drink!" *Coffee & Tea Industries,* Spices & Flavors, April 1963.

CHAPTER 5: THE SPECIALTY COFFEE BOOM

1   Adrian J. Slywotzky and Kevin Mundt, "Hold the Sugar; Starbucks Corp.'s Business Success," *Across the Board*, September 1996, 39.

2   Specialty Coffee Association of America and National Coffee Association, personal interviews, October 2005.

3   Information Resources, Inc., 2004.

4   Howard Schultz and Dori Jones Yang, *Pour Your Heart into It: How Starbucks Built a Company One Cup at a Time* (New York: Hyperion, 1997), 120–21.

5   Ray Oldenburg, *The Great Good Place* (New York: Paragon House, 1989), 296.

6   Faith Popcorn, *The Popcorn Report* (New York: HarperBusiness, 1992), 39–40.

7   Unscrupulous blending has also had a hand in this travesty—mixing a little genuine Kona into a Central American blend and calling it "Kona" or "Kona Blend."

8   The growth of the specialty coffee industry has also helped cultivate a rising demand for specialty teas, which, like coffees, focus on distinguishing themselves based on origin, cultivation, processing, and blending techniques. With most, if not all, of the specialty cafés in the country now offering a selection of specialty teas, the industry has expanded dramatically, with sales estimated at $1 billion for 2004. Steep growth in chai and organic tea, as well as fads like white tea, are helping drive this trend.

9   National Coffee Association, *National Coffee Drinking Trends Report*, 2004.

CHAPTER 6: THE SUSTAINABLE COFFEE BUZZ

1   Social Investment Forum Report, 1997.

2   Paul H. Ray, *The Integral Culture Survey: A Study of the Emergence of Transformational Values in America* (Sausalito, CA: Institute of Noetic Sciences and Kalamazoo, MI: Fetzer Institute, 1996).

3 John C. Ryan and Alan Thein Durning, *Stuff: The Secret Lives of Everyday Things* (Seattle, WA: Northwest Environment Watch, 1997), 7–12.

4 National Marketing Institute, "Organic Food and Beverage Sales Increase 18 Percent" Press release, February 22, 2005.

5 Datamonitor, "Natural Food and Drinks Report," 2003.

6 Paul H. Ray, *The Cultural Creatives: How 50 Million People Are Changing the World* (New York: Harmony Books, 2000).

7 Natural Marketing Institute, 2005. Corporate Social Responsibility, Consumer Understanding and Influence. Press release, August 18, 2005.

8 Giovannucci, D. "Sustainable Coffee Survey of the North American Specialty Coffee Industry," 2001.

9 National Coffee Association, personal interview with Joe DeRupo, Director of Communications and Public Relations, September 20, 2005.

10 SPINS, personal interview with David Browne, Director of Content Development, September 28, 2005.

11 National Coffee Association, "National Coffee Drinking Trends Report," 2005.

12 Interviewed by TransFair USA, January, 2005.

13 Peter Fritsch, "An Oversupply of Coffee Beans Deepens Latin America's Woes," *Wall Street Journal*, July 8, 2002.

14 Fair Trade Federation, "Fair Trade Trends Report," 2005.

15 Chris Willie, "The Birds and the Beans; Coffee Trees as Bird Habitats," *Audubon* 96, no. 6 (November 1994): 58.

Bibliography

Books of this type have been written many times before. As early as the seventeenth century, French, and later English, treatises on coffee attest to its compelling allure among writers. These treatises have appeared at regular intervals throughout the centuries, culminating in the epic *All About Coffee* in 1922. William Ukers, its author, has been cited by almost every subsequent coffee writer, and we are no exception. Like us, Ukers was a self-made writer. With only a high school diploma, young Ukers moved from his native Philadelphia to New York City, where he honed his editorial skills covering the coffee trade in the commercial center around Wall Street. In 1901, at thirty years of age, Ukers started his own trade journal. An inveterate workaholic, he was known worldwide as a living coffee encyclopedia, and his writings have become somewhat canonical, codifying some otherwise murky aspects of coffee history, such as the story of Francisco de Mello Palheta's role in the introduction of coffee to Brazil. Ukers's journal has matured into a worldwide source for coffee industry information, and his book is still found on the shelves of coffee people all over the world. This *Tea and Coffee Trade Journal* has been a major source for us, as have newer coffee journals such as *Fresh Cup*.

Because coffee is such a wide-ranging topic, we have used an eclectic range of literature, as well as numerous interviews and websites. For the bulk of our statistics, we have relied on the comprehensive raw data available from the Food and Agriculture Organization, as well as more U.S.–specific information from the National Coffee Association and the Specialty Coffee Association of America. The NCA's National Coffee Drinking Trends report was particularly valuable. Dating back to 1950, the NCA's Winter Coffee Drinking Survey is the premier source for U.S. consumption information, and is the reason why so much coffee writing contains the qualifier "on a given winter day." We were also fortunate to have the wealth of historical documents and rare texts of UC Berkeley's Bransten Coffee and Tea Collection at our disposal. Joseph M. Bransten was the B in the MJB coffee brand.

People we interviewed or otherwise discussed the world of coffee with include:

Jerry Baldwin, Peet's Coffee and Tea

Andrea Bass, Chock full o' Nuts

Shallom Berkman, Urth Caffé

Bob Bregenzer, Information Resources Inc.

David Browne, SPINS

Kevin Carothers, Starbucks

David Carrol, Guatemala News and Information Bureau

John Cossette, Royal Coffee

Michael Crawford, Prudential Securities

Paula De La Espedrilla, National Federation of Coffee
    Growers of Columbia (FNC)

Michael Del Gatto, Barrie House Coffee Co.

Joe DeRupo, National Coffee Association

Joe Dudeck, Information Resources, Inc.

Jan Eno, Thanksgiving Coffee Company

Mike Ferguson, Specialty Coffee Association of America

Bob Fulmer, Royal Coffee

Chris Gimble, Starbucks

Terence Gordon, Coffee, Sugar, and Cocoa Exchange of
    New York

David Griswold, Sustainable Harvest

Ben Harrison, Appropriate Technologies International

Paul Katzeff, Thanksgiving Coffee Company

Aaron Kiel, Specialty Coffee Association of America

Andrew Mastrangelo, Dunkin' Donuts

Jane McCabe, Tea & Coffee Trade Journal

Bruce McKinnon, Equal Exchange

Robert Nelson, National Coffee Association

Rodney North, Equal Exchange

Matt Quinlan, Conservation International

Paul Rice, TransFair USA

Robert Rice, Smithsonian Migratory Bird Center

Sabrina Rodriguez, Rainforest Alliance

Peter Rosset, Institute for Food and Development Policy

Luis Fernando Sampér, National Federation of Coffee
    Growers of Colombia (FNC)

Kim Seamen, Rainforest Alliance

Chris Shepherd, Café Altura

Donn Soares, Kauai Coffee Company

Margaret Swallow, Coffee Quality Institute

Gary Talboy, Specialty Coffee Consultants

Adam Teitelbaum, Adam's Organic Coffees

Martin Wattam, International Coffee Organization

Jeff Weinstein, Peet's Coffee and Tea

Doug Welsh, Peet's Coffee and Tea

Carla White, Specialty Coffee Association of America

Randy Wirth, Caffè Ibis

The following literature is listed in alphabetical order for
the chapter in which it is first used. Sources also used in
subsequent chapters are listed only in their first instance.
Minor sources are not listed.

CHAPTER I: A BRIEF HISTORY OF COFFEE

Bach, Johann Sebastian. *Coffee Cantata*. Leipzig, 1734.

Bradley, Richard. *The Virtue and Use of Coffee, with Regard
    to the Plague, and Other Infectious Distempers*. London:
    E. Mathews and W. Mears, 1721.

Bibliography

Bradshaw, Steve. *Café Society: Bohemian Life from Swift to Bob Dylan*. London: Weidenfeld and Nicolson, 1978.

Elector of Cologne, Maximillian Frederick, Bishop of Munster, Duchy of Westphalia, *Manifesto of February 17, 1784.*

Gray, Arthur. *Over the Black Coffee*. New York: The Baker and Taylor Company, 1902.

Heise, Ulla. *Coffee and Coffeehouses*. Translated by Paul Roper. Pennsylvania: Schiffer Publishing Ltd., 1987.

Jacob, Heinrich Eduard. *Coffee, the Epic of a Commodity*. Translated by Eden and Cedar Paul. New York: The Viking Press, 1935.

Kolpas, Norman. *Coffee*. London: John Murray (pubs), 1977.

The Men's Answer to the Women's Petition Against Coffee. London, 1674.

Mintz, Sidney W. *Sweetness and Power: The Place of Sugar in Modern History*. New York: Elisabeth Sifton Books/Viking, 1985.

Moseley, Benjamin. *Treatise Concerning the Properties and Effects of Coffee*. London: Printed for the author and sold by John Stockdale opposite Burlington House, 1785.

Nevill, Ralph. *Clubs: Their History and Treasures*. London: Chatto and Windus, 1911.

Robinson, Edward Forbes. *The Early History of Coffeehouses in England*. London: Kegan Paul, Trench, Trüber & Co., Ltd., 1893.

Schapira, J. and K. Schapira. *The Book of Coffee and Tea*. New York: St. Martin's Press, 1975.

Schivelbusch, Wolfgang. *Tastes of Paradise: A Social History of Spices, Stimulants, and Intoxicants*. New York: Pantheon Books, 1992.

Smith, R. F. "A History of Coffee." In *Coffee: Botany, Biochemistry, and Production*, edited by M. N. Clifford and K. C. Wilson. Beckenham Australia: Croon Helm Ltd., 1985.

Syers, R. *The Coffee Guide; For the Use of Purchasers, Preparers, and Consumers*. London: David Marples and Richard Taylor and Hamilton, Adams, and Co., 1832.

Ukers, William H. *All About Coffee*, 2nd ed. New York: The Tea & Coffee Trade Journal Company, 1935.

Weatherstone, John. *The Pioneers: 1825–1900*. London: Quiller Press, Ltd., 1986.

Wild, Antony. *Coffee: A Dark History*. New York: W. W. Norton, 2004.

The Women's Petition Against Coffee. London, 1674.

CHAPTER 2: COFFEE'S ODYSSEY FROM CROP TO CUP

Barry, Tom. *Roots of Rebellion*. Boston: South End Press, 1987.

CIA *Factbook*. 1997, 2005.

Clark, Robert, ed. *Our Sustainable Table*. San Francisco: North Point Press, 1990.

Clarke, R. J. and R. Macrae, eds. *Coffee. Volume 4: Agronomy*. London: Elsevier Applied Science, 1985.

Coffee & Tea Store. A&A Business Manual #1202. Entrepreneurs Inc., Irvine, CA, 1991.

Heuman, John. "Coffee in the Spotlight: Always Walking a Tight Rope," *Coffee Annual 1994*, March 1995.

Illy, Andreas and Rinantonio Viani, eds. *Espresso Coffee: The Chemistry of Quality*. San Diego: Academic Press Ltd., 1995.

Janssen, Rivers, "Making Sense of Sustainability," *Fresh Cup*, January 1997.

Knox, K. and J. S. Huffaker. *Coffee Basics*. New York: John Wiley & Sons, Inc., 1997.

Luxner, Larry, "Febec President Oswaldo Aranha Neto Speaks Out," *Tea & Coffee Trade Journal* 168, no. 7 (July 1996).

Madray, William G. "Crisis 1976," *Coffee Annual 1976*, February 1977.

McClumpha, A. D. "The Trading of Green Coffee." In *Coffee. Volume 6: Commercial and Technico-Legal Aspects*, edited by R. J. Clarke and R. Macrae. London: Elsevier Applied Science, 1988.

Navarro, Luis Hernandez. "Coffee: A Virtual Fiefdom." In *Proceedings of the First Sustainable Coffee Congress*, edited by R. A. Rice, A. M. Harris, and J. McLean. Washington DC: Smithsonian Migratory Bird Center, 1997.

North London Haslemere Group. *Coffee: The Rules of Neocolonialism*. London: Third World First, 1972.

Parke, Gertrude. *The Big Coffee Cookbook*. New York: Funk & Wagnalls, 1969.

Pelini, Patrick. "Putting a Face to Coffee: Part One." *North Country News*, March 1996.

Pennybacker, Mindy, "Habitat-saving Habit; Shaded Coffee Plantations Help Preserve Tropical Rainforests," *Sierra* 82, no. 2 (March 1997): 18.

Perfecto, I., R. Rice, R. Greenberg, and M. E. Van der Voort. "Shade Coffee: A Disappearing Refuge for Biodiversity." *Bioscience* 46, no. 8 (1996): 598–608.

Preston, John. "Quality Progress Stimulates Instant Coffee, Tea Usage." *Coffee & Tea Industries, Spices & Flavors*, July 1963.

Raudales, Raul A. "Encouraging Sustainable Coffee: Technologies, Economics, Policies." In *Proceedings of the First Sustainable Coffee Congress*, edited by R. A. Rice, A. M. Harris, and J. McLean. Washington, DC: Smithsonian Migratory Bird Center, 1997.

Rice, Robert A., Ashley M. Harris, and Jennifer McLean, eds. *Proceedings of the First Sustainable Coffee Congress.* Washington, DC: Smithsonian Migratory Bird Center, 1997.

Rice, R. and J. Ward. "From Shade to Sun: The Industrialization of Coffee Production," *Global Pesticide Campaigner* 7, no. 3 (September 1997).

Schoenholt, Donald. "Slurping and Spitting in the Twentieth-Century; Coffee Drinking; Coffee Cupping Report." *Tea & Coffee Trade Journal*, February 1995.

Smith, Jim. "Traditional Warehousing Operations Expected to Prevail." *Tea & Coffee Trade Journal*, December 1996.

Smithsonian Migratory Bird Center. *Why Migratory Birds Are Crazy for Coffee.* Washington, DC, 1997.

Swasy, Alecia. *Soap Opera: The Inside Story of Procter & Gamble.* New York: Times Books, 1993.

Talbot, John M. *Ground for Agreement: The Political Economy of the Coffee Commodity Chain.* Oxford: Rowman & Littlefield, 2004.

Talbot, John M. "The Struggle for Control of a Commodity Chain: Instant Coffee from Latin America." *Latin American Research Review* 32, no. 2 (1997): 117–35.

Talbot, John M. "Where Does Your Coffee Dollar Go? The Division of Income and Surplus along the Coffee Commodity Chain." *Studies in Comparative International Development* 32, no. 1 (1997): 56–91.

Thorn, Jon. *The Coffee Companion.* Philadelphia: Running Press, 1995.

Thurber, Francis B. *Coffee: From Plantation to Cup. A Brief History of Coffee Production and Consumption with an Appendix containing letters written during a trip to the coffee plantations of the East, and through the coffee consuming countries of Europe.* New York: American Grocer Publishing Association, 1884.

Uribe, Andrés C. *Brown Gold: The Amazing Story of Coffee.* New York: Random House, 1954.

Wallengren, Maja. "Costa Rica's Coffee Heading for Change." *Tea & Coffee Trade Journal* 170, no. 2 (February 1998): 45–46.

CHAPTER 3: THE RISE OF THE INTERNATIONAL
COFFEE TRADE

Bates, Robert H. *Open-Economy Politics: The Political Economy of the World Coffee Trade*. Princeton: Princeton University Press, 1997.

de Graaf, J. *The Economics of Coffee*. Wageningen, Netherlands: Center for Agricultural Publishing and Documentation (Pudoc), 1986.

Food and Agriculture Organization. *Commodity Review and Outlook / FAOSTAT Database*. Rome, 1986–2005.

Furtado, Celso. *The Economic Growth of Brazil: A Survey from Colonial to Modern Times*. Berkeley: University of California Press, 1965.

Remarks by Senator Hubert Humphrey, U.S. Senate, 88th Congress, 1st Session, *Congressional Record*. May 20, 1963, 8552.

International Coffee Organization. *Basic Information: Objectives, Structure, History, and Operation*. London: International Coffee Organization, 1996.

Luxner, Larry. "Colombian Coffee Federation President Speaks Out." *Tea and Coffee Trade Journal* 169, no. 7 (July 1997): 13–17.

Maizels, Alfred, Robert Bacon, and George Mavrotas. *Commodity Supply Management by Producing Countries: A Case Study of the Tropical Beverage Crops*. Oxford: Clarendon Press, 1997.

Marshall, C. F. "World Coffee Trade." In *Coffee: Botany, Biochemistry, and Production of Beans and Beverage*, edited by M. N. Clifford and K. C. Wilson. Beckenham, Australia: Croom Helm Ltd., 1985.

Meono, Charles, ed. Editorial. *Coffee & Tea Industries* 85, no. 2 (February 1962).

Ministry of Agriculture, Industry & Commerce. *Coffee; Edition of the Coffee Institute of the State of São Paulo*. Rio de Janeiro, 1928.

Gresser, Charis, and Sophia Tickell. *Mugged: Poverty in Your Coffee Cup*. Boston: Oxfam International, 2002.

Paige, Jeffrey M. *Coffee and Power: Revolution and the Rise of Democracy in Central America*. Cambridge: Harvard University Press, 1997.

Pan-American Coffee Bureau. *Coffee and the U.S. Consumer*. New York: 1 April, 1964.

Peel, Carl. "The Brazilian Influence." *Tea & Coffee Trade Journal* 169, no. 7 (July 1997): 26–34.

Pendergrast, Mark. *Uncommon Grounds: The History of Coffee and How It Transformed Our World*. New York: Basic Books, 1999.

Short, Joseph. *American Business and Foreign Policy: Cases in Coffee and Cocoa Trade Regulation 1961–1974*. New York: Garland Publishing, Inc., 1987.

Vaughan, Lisa. "Producers Sign Coffee Pact." *The Independent*, August 23, 1993.

CHAPTER 4: HEALTH, MARKETING, AND THE
MEGA-ROASTERS

Bennet, Stephen, "Beverages; Supermarket Beverage Sales; 1989 Supermarket Sales Manual," *Progressive Grocer*, July 1989.

Bergh, Chip. "Folgers." Presentation to the National Coffee Association Convention, March 20, 1998.

Brody, Jane E. "The Latest on Coffee? Don't Worry. Drink Up." *New York Times*, September 13, 1995.

Coffee & Tea Industries. *Coffee and Chemistry*, July 1962, 39–40.

Consumers Union of United States, Inc., "Coffee and Health." *Consumer Reports*, October 1994.

Davids, Kenneth. *The Coffee Book*. Weybridge: Whittet Books, 1980.

Garattini, Silvio. *Caffeine, Coffee, and Health*. New York: Raven Press, 1993.

Janssen, Rivers. "Appellation." *Fresh Cup*, October 1997.

Kimura, Takayoshi. "Coffee in Japan—1994." *Coffee Annual 1994*, March 1995.

Kuhn, Cynthia, Scott Schwartzwelder, and Wilkie Wilson. *Buzzed*. New York: W. W. Norton and Co., 1998.

McDowell, Bill. "The Bean Counters." *Restaurants & Institutions*, December 1995.

McKenna, Terence. *Food of the Gods*. New York: Bantam Books, 1992.

National Coffee Association. *Winter Drinking Survey*. New York: National Coffee Association, 2005.

Oldenburg, Ray. *The Great Good Place*. New York: Paragon House, 1989.

Peel, Carl. "Los Angeles, a Microcosm of the Country." *Tea and Coffee Trade Journal* 169, no. 4 (April 1997): 16–28.

Popcorn, Faith. *The Popcorn Report*. New York: HarperBusiness, 1992.

Quinn, James P., *Scientific Marketing of Coffee*. New York: Tea & Coffee Trade Journal Co., 1960.

Schisgall, Oscar. *Eyes on Tomorrow: The Evolution of Procter & Gamble*. New York: J. G. Ferguson Publishing Company, 1981.

Schultz, Howard and Dori Jones Yang. *Pour Your Heart Into It: How Starbucks Built a Company One Cup at a Time*. New York: Hyperion, 1997.

Slywotzky, Adrian J. and Kevin Mundt. "Hold the Sugar; Starbucks Corp.'s Business Success." *Across the Board*, September 1996.

Struning, William C. "The Life Cycle of Coffee in the USA." *Coffee Annual* 1993, February 1994.

Tansey, Geoff and Tony Worsley. *The Food System: A Guide*. London: Earthscan Publications, Ltd., 1995.

Tea and Coffee Trade Journal (staff report), "Kona Coffee Scandal: Kona Kai Farms Implicated." *Tea and Coffee Trade Journal* 169, no. 1 (January 1997): 13–21.

White, Nick, EVP Food Team. "Wal-Mart." Presentation to the National Coffee Association Convention, March 21, 1998.

U.S./Guatemala Labor Education Campaign Update, April 1998.

Waridel, Laure. *Coffee With a Cause*. Montréal: Les Éditions des Intouchables, 1997.

Wille, Chris. "The birds and the beans; coffee trees as bird habitats," *Audubon*, November 1994.

CHAPTER 6: THE SUSTAINABLE COFFEE BUZZ

CHAPTER 5: THE SPECIALTY COFFEE BOOM

Bird, Laura. *Wall Street Journal*, December 14, 1995, cited on Fair Trade Federation website.

Carrol, John, ed. *Making Coffee Strong: Alternative Trading in a Conventional World*. Canton, Massachusetts: Equal Exchange, 1994.

Equal Exchange. Company information materials. 1998–2005.

Equal Exchange. *Java Jive: A Quarterly Newsletter on Fair Trade and Equal Exchange* 17, August 1997.

Fair Trade Federation website (www.fairtrade federation.com), April 22, 1998.

Raimy, Eric. "Caffeine Nation." *Human Resource Executive*, March 1996.

Ryan, John C., and Alan Thein Durning. *Stuff: The Secret Lives of Everyday Things*. Seattle, WA: Northwest Environment Watch, 1997.

Lewin, B., D. Giovannucci, and P. Varangis. "Coffee Markets: New Paradigms in Supply and Demand," World Bank, 2004.

Nichols, Alex, and Charlotte Opal. *Fair Trade: Market-Driven Ethical Consumption*. London: SAGE Publications, 2005.

Image Credits

We are grateful for permission to use the following materials:

Page 4: Illustration of Kaldi, from *All About Coffee* by William Ukers, reprinted by permission of the Tea and Coffee Trade Journal.

Page 14: Lloyd's Coffee House illustration by permission of Lloyd's of London.

Page 32: Illustration of the King's Arms, from *All About Coffee* by William Ukers, reprinted by permission of the Tea and Coffee Trade Journal.

Page 40: Zee Beeg Coffee illustration by Steve Curl reprinted by permission of Steve Curl. © 1998 by Steve Curl.

Page 46: Photograph of farmer picking coffee by Janet Jarman. Reprinted by permission of Janet Jarman. © 2004 by Janet Jarman.

Page 64: Photograph of coffee drying by Derril Bazzy. Reprinted by permission of Derril Bazzy. © 1998 by Derril Bazzy.

Page 67: Photograph of farmers cupping coffee in Nicaragua by Janet Jarman. Reprinted by permission of Janet Jarman. © 2004 by Janet Jarman.

Page 79: Angola coffee advertisement reprinted by permission of the Angola Instituto Nacionál Do Café.

Page 144: Chock full o' Nuts advertisement reprinted by permission of Chock full o' Nuts.

Page 157: Photograph of espresso-shot by Gregory Dicum.

Page 172: Photograph of cappuccino by Gregory Dicum.

Page 182: Espresso represso cartoon by Joe Hoover, originally published in the Highland Villager, St. Paul, Minnesota. Reprinted by permission of Joe Hoover. © 1994 by Joe Hoover.

Page 198: "Willful exploitation" cartoon reprinted by permission of Equal Exchange.

Page 209: Photograph of coffee in store by Nina Luttinger.

Index